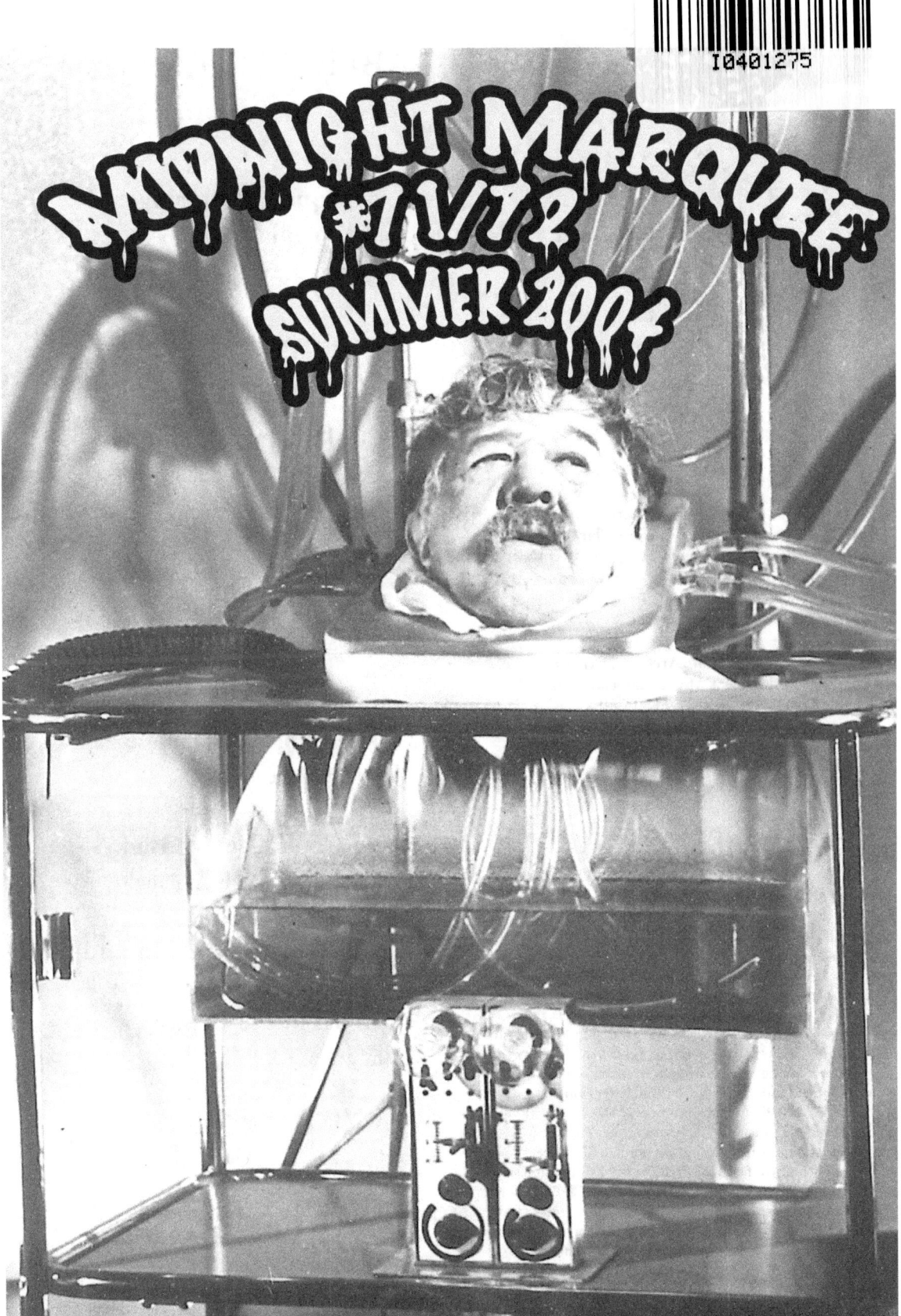

MIDNIGHT MARQUEE
Number 70/71

Editors
Gary J. Svehla
Susan Svehla

Managing Editor
Richard J. Svehla

Copy Editor
Scott A. Nollen

Graphic Design Interior
Susan Svehla

Cover Design/ Title Page Design
Susan Svehla

Contributing Writers
Anthony Ambrogio, Mark Clark, Jonathan M. Lampley, Arthur Lennig, Michael H. Price, Cindy Collins Smith, Brian Smith, Bryan Senn, Gary J. Svehla, Steven Thornton, Robert Tinnell

Acknowledgments
John Antosiewicz Photo Archives, Eric Caidin, Jerry Ohlinger's Movie Material Store, John E. Parnum Archival Collection Photofest/Buddy Weiss, Michael H. Price

Illustrator
Allen J. Koszowski

Publisher
Midnight Marquee Press

Midnight Marquee
Number 70/71
Copyright 2004 © by Gary J. Svehla
  Published twice yearly by Midnight Marquee Press at $17 per year. Printed by Boyd Printing, Albany, NY.
  Return postage must accompany articles and art, if the owner wants them returned. No responsibility is taken for unsolicited material. Editorial views expressed by our contributors are not necessarily those of the publisher. Nothing may be reproduced in any media without written permission of the publisher. Send submissions of articles, letters and art to Gary J. Svehla, 9721 Britinay Lane, Baltimore, MD 21234; web site: http://www.midmar.com; e-mail: mmarquee@aol.com
  Letters of comment addressed to Midnight Marquee or Gary or Susan Svehla will be considered for publication unless the writer requests otherwise. Subscription rates: $10 per single copy or $17 per year (shipped U.S. Media Mail). Subscription copies are mailed in sturdy cardboard mailers and will arrive in excellent condition; support MidMar by becoming a direct-mail subscriber. Foreign orders are $39 (U.S.) for a two issue subscription.

TABLE OF CONTENTS

3 **Marquee Mutterings: Editorial**
by Gary J. Svehla

4 **Say Awwwww! Mad Doctor Mania**

15 **2001's Cinematic Relativity**
by Arthur Joseph Lundquist

23 *Homicidal*—**William Castle's Slice and Dice Job**
by David J. Hogan

32 **D.W. Griffith's Avenging Conscience**
by Arthur Lennig

37 **So Good They're Bad**
Edited by Anthony Ambrogio

50 **150 Years of Women and Horror: She Has Always Lived in the Castle**
by James J.J. Janis

64 **DVD Reviews**
by Gary J. Svehla

94 **Grave Diggings [Letters]**

Marquee Mutterings

Sorry for the lateness of the issue, but with the debut of our third magazine, *Movie Mystique*, we have been overwhelmed. Time is always the enemy when there are only two people in the office, so thank you for your patience.

Even though technically the Fox TV series *24* is not in the horror-science fiction genre, its weekly plot riddled with madmen, terrorists, viral attacks upon the major US cities and even the old ploy of using an axe to sever an agent's wrist/arm (a deadly virus is attached to the arm with a timer, which will release itself in aerosol form in less than a minute) is the type of stuff that belongs in the horror/science fiction genre. Ending its third year this past May, *24* has proven to be my favorite TV series since *Twin Peaks* appeared over a decade ago. I never miss an episode and find myself riveted to the TV screen every Tuesday night at 9 p.m. (drat, next year's fourth season does not begin until January and it will now be seen Monday nights at 9). For those who missed the first two seasons, the entire first season *Day 1* and second season *Day 2* are now available as DVD boxed sets and probably by late summer *Day 3* (this third season) will also be available. For gripping suspense, tightly woven multiple plots and some wonderful performances (Keifer Sutherland simply shines as agent Jack Bauer, becoming the glue that holds all the interconnected plot threads together), *24* is classic television. With each hour episode ending in a nail-biting cliffhanger, *24* becomes the modern era's equivalent of the old Republic serial, with each serial consisting of 24 chapters lasting roughly 45 minutes instead of 12 or 15 chapters lasting 20 minutes. *24* is aimed at adult sensibilities and not the Saturday matinee crowd, so whenever I see jet aircraft shoot missiles at enemy helicopters or watch transfixed as agent Bauer assassinates his colleague and superior by shooting him in the back of the head—the agent on his knees pleading for his life—well, I realize television seldom gets more intense. Catch *24* on DVD if you missed the first three seasons, and stay tuned for *Day 4* premiering next January. Once you are hooked, you will stay hooked.

I generally hate movies that are manufactured to become cult/B movies—such as *Attack of the Killer Tomatoes*, *Killer Klowns from Outer Space* or *The Toxic Avenger*—because filmmakers work too hard to produce something that appeared quite naturally during the decade of the 1950s. When Ed Wood directed *Bride of the Monster* or *Plan 9 From Outer Space*, he was making serious science fiction/horror programmers the best he knew how. He was not trying to produce the worst movie ever made, nor was he laughing at or spoofing better genre productions. He was simply trying to create entertainment on a non-existent budget. That's why I am much more sympathetic toward Larry Blamire's *The Lost Skeleton of Cadavra*, an independent movie Blamire, his wife and friends made and released two years ago in 2002 (and just now released to DVD). As was stressed in the cast/crew Q&A during the film's premiere, *The Lost Skeleton of Cadavra* was not produced to spoof the low-budget B productions of the 1950s; it was produced to *be* a B production. Filmed in less than a week in Bronson Canyon and other locations, the movie was shot digitally and printed in black and white. True, at 90 minutes the paper-thin plot is stretched pretty thin, but the stereotyped American scientist who is adored by his Stepford housewife simply lays the groundwork for other interesting 1950s stereotypes to sustain viewer interest: the feline *Cat Women of the Moon* inspired Animala (played by Blamire's wife Jennifer Blaire), Ranger Brad (Don Conroy) and alien Kro-Bar (Andrew Parks) all play deadpan character roles that are lovingly crafted from the B era of the 1950s. Throw in some crazy dancing, add a plastic skeleton whose black wires are plainly visible and introduce a mutant that comes directly from the school of design of *Horror of Party Beach*, and we have an homage that generally does justice to this bygone era (even down to some embarrassingly bad acting, sequences that drag on a tad too long and sequences that have way too much talk and far too little action). As stated, *The Lost Skeleton of Cadavra* is flawed yet fun (as were the plethora of movies that inspired the film) and it is definitely must-see viewing for any fan of the nadir of 1950s low-budget science fiction cinema. I must admit the movie entertained.

Amazingly, the independent horror movie craze of the 1970s has returned with a vengeance 25 years later with remakes of *The Texas Chainsaw Massacre*, *Dawn of the Dead* and recent tributes to that era with *House of 1000 Corpses*, *Wrong Turn*, *28 Days Later*, *Cabin Fever*, etc. Such a wealth of horror genre entries over the course of the past two years has lead to a mini resurgence of the genre. And surprisingly, most of these movies have been produced with style and finesse. Go back and look at original movies such as *The Hills Have Eyes*. Some don't hold up too well and already seem dated. Most of the remakes have been done with major Hollywood financing with much larger budgets than the originals could even dream of, yet the results are seldom overblown or embarrassing. Of course, when it comes to redoing the original Universal horror classics, we get the CGI overkill of *Van Helsing*, a movie not without its own merits. New remakes of *The Blob* are also promised. While it may seem that such remakes are coming much too soon, it must be remembered that Universal started its classic horror cycle in 1931 and by 1956 Hammer was already releasing Technicolor remakes of classic Frankenstein and Count Dracula movies only 25 years after the originals played theatrically. So amazingly, remakes of 1970s movies appearing 25 years later are no different than what Hammer did 50 years ago. The greater question should be: Why remake these movies and have they found a new audience to make such productions financially feasible? The damn shame is that George Romero is trying to obtain financing to film a fourth installment of the his zombie series that started with *Night of the Living Dead* in 1968, and instead of giving the originator the money he needs, producers instead film a remake of *Dawn of the Dead*. I think we first need to hear the final word from Romero before we worry about remaking films that aren't exactly screaming out to be remade.

See everyone again in about six months!

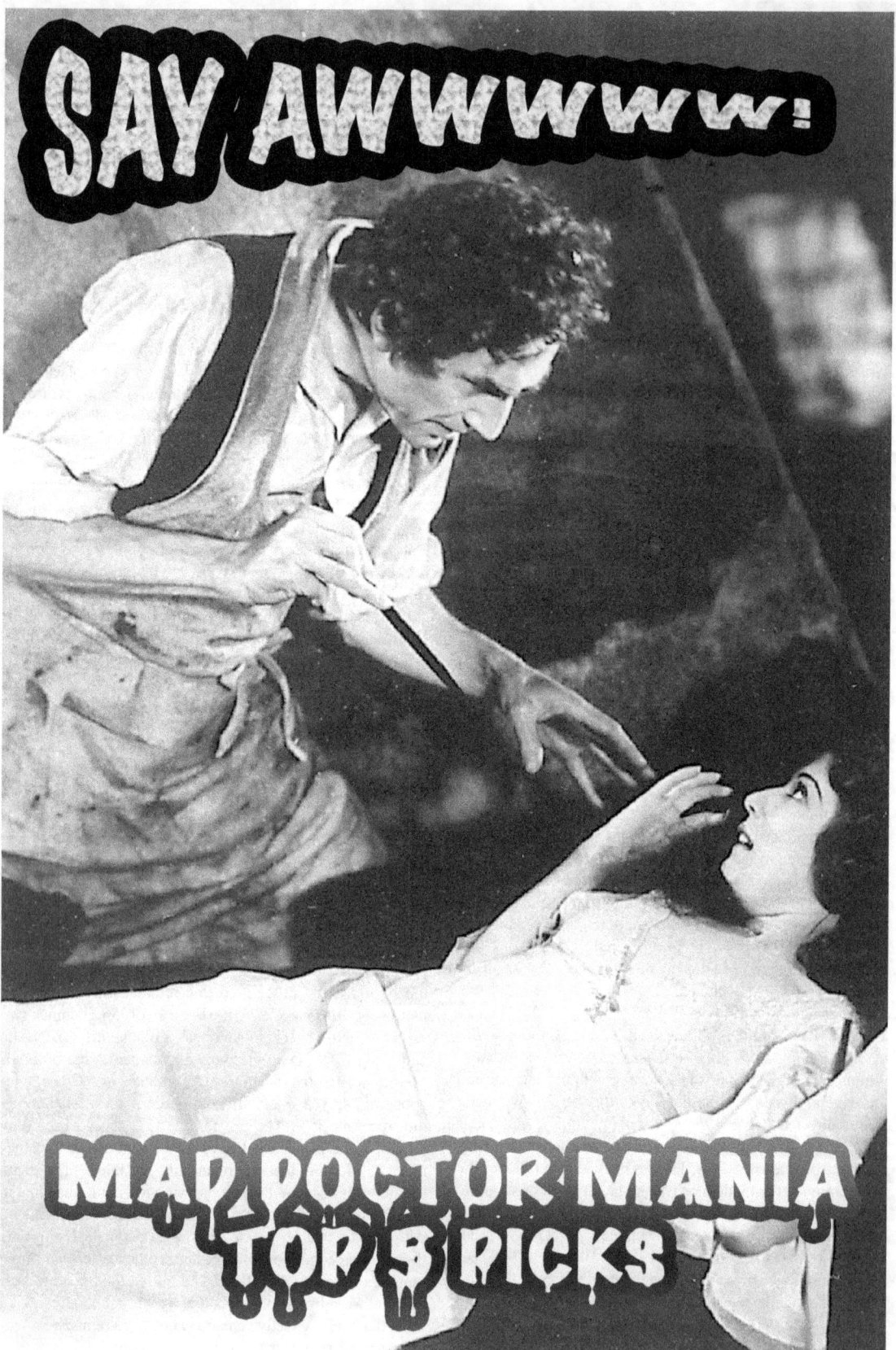

My Favorite Mad Doctors:
1. Boris Karloff as Dr. Niemann in *House of Frankenstein*: "Now friend Daniel, Frankenstein would have severed the spinal cord here... but I'm not quite sure he was correct." Karloff was also great in *Frankenstein 1970*.
2. Bela Lugosi as Dr. Vornoff in *Bride of the Monster*: "Here in this forsaken jungle hell, Professor Strowsky, I have proved that I am all right!"
3. John Carradine as Dr. von Altermann in *Revenge of the Zombies*: "Ah—Hooooooo!"
4. Lionel Atwill as Dr. Ralph Benson in *The Mad Doctor of Market Street*: Atwill played mad docs in more movies than I can remember.
5. And finally... Horst Frank as Dr. Ood in The *Head*! Possibly the maddest doctor of them all!

All the above have provided inspiration and role models for us down through the years.
—Rockin' Lon Talbot

My top five favorite mad scientist flicks? Man, that's a toughie; so many to choose from! Here goes…
1. *The Devil Bat*—Who else but Bela Lugosi could turn an otherwise silly poverty row, no-budget PRC thriller into such an entertaining romp? Peppered with some classic mad scientist dialogue, *The Devil Bat* is raised from obscurity by Lugosi's over-the-top portrayal of Dr. Carruthers, an exploited scientist. Cheated and hung out to dry by a profiteering cosmetics firm (shades of Enron), Dr. Carruthers takes what he perceives to be justified revenge by turning his oppressors into walking guinea pigs with his giant bat-attracting aftershave. And nobody—nobody—could make a simple good-bye sound like such a death sentence!
2. *Frankenstein's Daughter*—This low rent cheesy movie features great portrayals. Mr. Frank's explanation of his elderly colleague's seemingly incredible behavior to the police is hilarious: "He's a little, well, you know."
3. *Die, Monster, Die*—Well past his prime in physical years (heck, he was already middle-aged when he got his vehicle role in *Frankenstein*), Boris Karloff is nevertheless at his prime in this movie. In the bedroom scene with his wife, Karloff's character sends chills of delight through the viewer's spine as he raises an eyebrow and says: "If there was evil, it was buried with him."
4. *Flesh for Frankenstein* (aka *Andy Warhol's Frankenstein*)—This is possibly Udo Kier's greatest career role. Chock-full of sexual weirdness, *Flesh For Frankenstein* is also a 3-D gore-fest. But never mind all that. Kier absolutely rocks!
5. *Bride of the Monster*—Long forgotten by the big shots at Universal and the other major Hollywood producers, Bela Lugosi delivers one of his swan song performances in Ed Wood's finest film. One final comeback attempt. One final good-bye. "Home... I have no home. Hunted. Despised. Living like an animal. The jungle is my home. But I will show the world that I can be its master. I will perfect my own race of people: a race of atomic supermen which will conquer the world!" Over the top. Played to the hilt. Pure Lugosi!
—Douglas Brown

1. Bela Lugosi
2. Lionel Atwill
3. George Zucco
4. Peter Lorre (Mad Love)
5. Boris Karloff
(And if I could be so presumptuous, could I add one more?)
6. Colin Clive
—Arthur Lennig

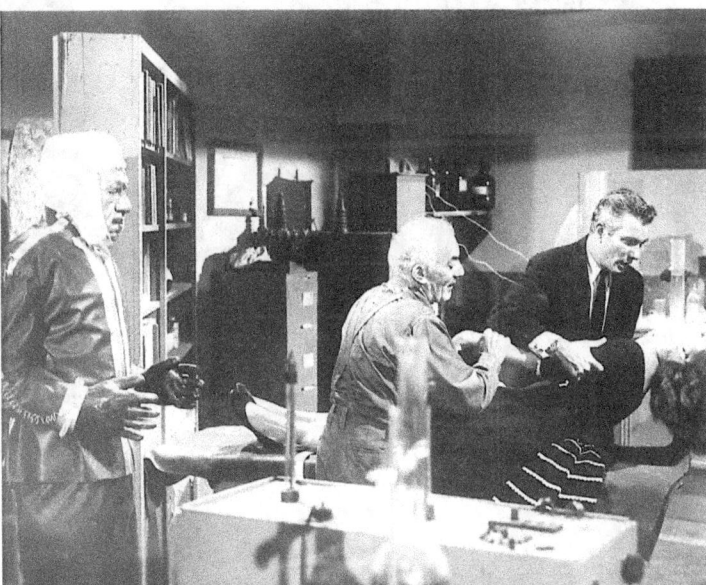
"He's a little, well, you know..." Medical mayhem in *Frankenstein's Daughter*

1. Bela Lugosi
2. Lionel Atwill
3. Boris Karloff
4. John Carradine
5. George Zucco
—Dr. Vollin, MD

Ultimate Mad Doctor Films:
1. *Metropolis* (1927): The ultimate evil scientist and his mad dream survive.
2. *Bride of Frankenstein* (1935): Why have one mad doctor when you can have two, each responsible for his own monster!

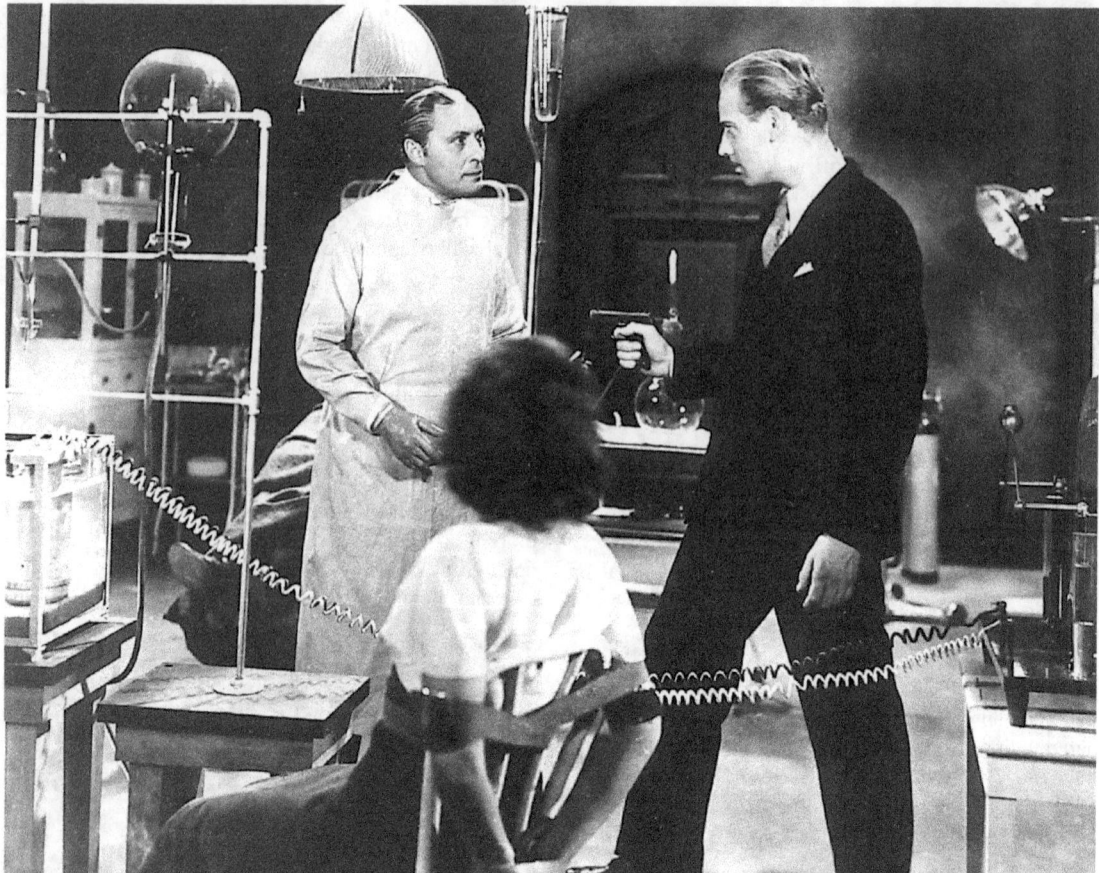

Lionel Atwill "had such malevolence in the 1930s and '40s as a mad doctor" in such films as *The Vampire Bat.*

3. *House of Dracula* (1945): The last Universal mad doctor (Onslow Stevens) is one of the best.
4. *Back to the Future* (1985): An homage to *Metropolis* with Christopher Lloyd's Dr. Brown?
5. *Young Frankenstein* (1974): Gene Wilder creates an unforgettable homage.
—Scott Essman

1. Lionel Atwill: *Man Made Monster, The Vampire Bat,* and *Ghost of Frankenstein.* No one had such malevolence in the 1930s and '40s as a mad doctor as Lionel Atwill. The only tragedy is he never had a definitive movie to play a mad doctor, but even just one of these is enough to get him on the top five list where he reigns as number one.
2. Colin Clive: Ultimately his Dr. Frankenstein is not as mad as Atwill's mad doctor, but just as devoted and maybe even more intense. Clive was the perfect man for the role in the Universal classics.
3. Boris Karloff: *The Man Who Changed His Mind* and many, many Columbia horror films. After 1935 Karloff seemed to play nothing but mad scientists. He was good in nearly all of them and merits a place on this list.
4. Bela Lugosi: *Murders in the Rue Morgue, The Raven, Dark Eyes of London, The Devil Bat.* Lugosi was absolutely splendid and uniquely different in each of these four films. Lugosi was actually a terrifically underrated mad doctor.
5. George Zucco: *The Mad Ghoul, Dr. Renault's Secret.* Zucco was extremely disturbing in *The Mad Ghoul*, lending that film its true moments of horror. He was also excellent in the supremely underrated *Dr. Renault's Secret.*
—Kenny Strong

1. Peter Cushing as Baron Frankenstein: Over the course of six films, Cushing so memorably defined Mary Shelley's Faustian protagonist that it is almost impossible to accept anyone else in the role. By turns heroic and evil, Cushing's Frankenstein is a fascinating study in the evolution of a role over the course of many years and movies. The conclusion of *Frankenstein and the Monster from Hell,* in which the character is revealed to be wholly insane, is shocking and even a little pathetic. Cushing is great in all of these films, but if I had to pick just one, I would have to go for his most sympathetic turn in the criminally underappreciated *Evil of Frankenstein* (1964).
2. Vincent Price as Dr. Anton Phibes in *The Abominable Dr. Phibes* (1971): Billed as Price's 100th film (it wasn't), *The Abominable Dr. Phibes* gave the noted horror star a new kind of part to play in the autumn of his career—the wronged maniac who avenges himself on his foes in bi-

zarrely comic ways. Dr. Phibes is neither a medico nor a scientist—he's an academic, with dual doctorates in music and theology. This is an interesting variation on the stereotype, and Price mines the film for every laugh. My favorite of his bits takes place after Phibes drains Dr. Longstreet (Terry-Thomas) of his blood: Phibes lingers to cast a disparaging eye towards one of Longstreet's paintings in a great reference to Price's well-known expertise in art.

3. Jeffrey Combs as Herbert West in *Re-Animator* (1986): "You'll never get credit for my discoveries. Who'd believe a talking head? Get a job in a sideshow!" With that line, Jeffrey Combs immediately made my list of the cinema's maddest scientists. *Re-Animator* is a lot bloodier—and funnier—than the original Lovecraft serial that inspired the movie. It's also more entertaining than the group of stories ol' HPL himself ranked near the bottom of his output, and much of that fun factor is due to Combs' over-the-top performance as Herbert West.

4. Anthony Hopkins as Dr. Hannibal Lecter in *The Silence of the Lambs* (1991): It is probably an overdone choice, but what can I say? Hopkins won a well-deserved Oscar for his terrifying turn as the cannibalistic shrink; it's a performance that still works after more than a decade of sequels, rip-offs and parodies. The erudite and charming Dr. Lecter perfectly embodies the charm of evil that Terence Fisher used to go on about.

5. Fredric March as Dr. Henry Jekyll in *Dr. Jekyll and Mr. Hyde* (1932): The first time an actor won an Oscar for a horror part was also for portraying a mad doctor. True, March's Jekyll isn't quite insane, but his alter ego, the brutish Mr. Hyde, certainly is. Even after more than 70 years, March's acting still packs a punch. Furthermore, the film itself is scarier than almost any other shocker from the Golden Age.

—Jonathan M. Lampley

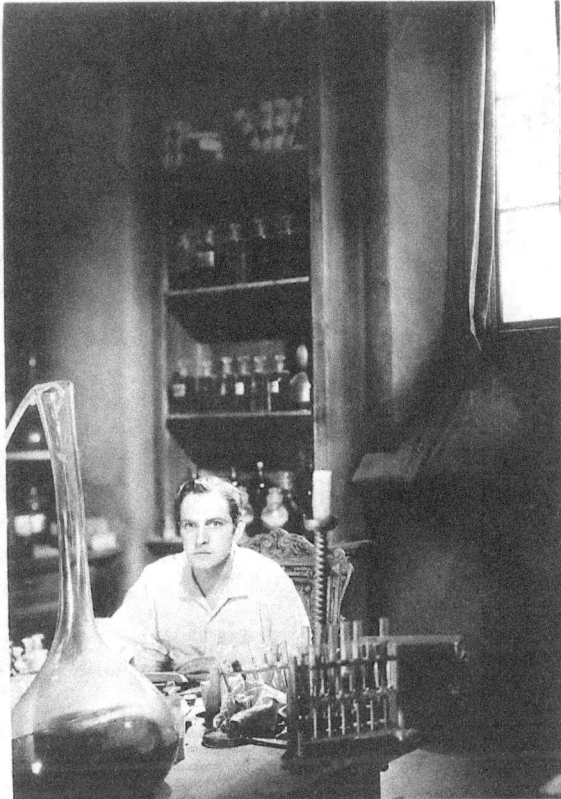

Fredric March won an Academy Award for his mad doctor portrayal of Dr. Jekyll.

In response to your request, here are my top-five favorite mad doctors:

1. Dr. Eric Vornoff: Bela's last speaking role in Ed Wood's miserable *Bride of the Monster* has always been one of my faves. Despite the threadbare surroundings, Lugosi gives one of his most enjoyable performances. And any doctor who thinks a photo enlarger will make one of his patients "as big as a giant, with the strength of 20 men" has to be mad!

2. Herbert West: Jeffrey Combs in *Re-Animator* delivers the first of many quirky performances that secured his position as one of the few (if only) current actors primarily identified with genre films. The movie is a memorably wild ride, and one of the best horror films of the 1980s.

Jeffrey Combs gets ahead in *Re-Animator!*

3. Dr. Pretorius: My all-time favorite horror film features one of the all-time best mad doctors. A practitioner of black magic, one wonders what else might have transpired in his "humble abode." I wish Ernest Thesiger had made a few more appearances in horror films of the 1930s (other than *The Ghoul* or *They Drive By Night*, 1938). Might he have topped his most macabre performance?

4. Professor Dexter: Bela Lugosi in *Return of the Ape Man* delivers one of the juiciest mad doctor lines of all time: "Some people's brains would never be missed." This mad doctor is worthy of consideration for that profound observation alone!

5. Dr. Moreau: Charles Laughton's performance in *Island of Lost Souls* reeks of sadism and debauchery and stands out as one of weirdest characterizations in all 1930s horror films (pre-Code or otherwise). He was definitely mad, and that's why he makes my list!

—Tom Shumaker

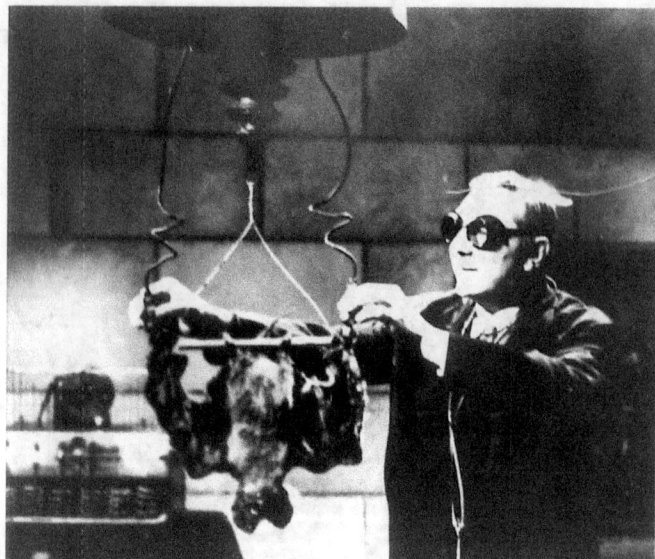

Bela Lugosi as the revenge seeking Dr. Paul Carruthers in *The Devil Bat*.

1. I just have to mention a favorite mad doctor scene. In *Doctor X*, with Lionel Atwill and Fay Wray, there is a scene with Preston Foster in which he transforms into the midnight killer while chanting "synthetic flesh, synthetic flesh!" That must be one of the best mad lab scenes ever.

   Okay, four more...
2. Peter Lorre in *Mad Love*. He is just so eye-bugging mad.
3. Colin Clive, for both his performances as Dr. Frankenstein. He is so wired. He would be a great mad doctor even if he did not happen to be re-animating dead tissue.
4. Rotwang from *Metropolis*... I had to mention at least one German expressionist mad doctor.
5. I almost forgot to mention Ernest Thesiger as Dr. Pretorius... "Gin, it's my only weakness." This is my top six list.
6. Last but not least: Dr. Jekyll in the 1932 version of *Dr. Jekyll and Mr. Hyde* with Fredric March. That film had the classic combination of great mad lab scenes and a scientist who is a genius (but still thinks it might be smart to use himself as a test subject). March is my favorite Mr. Hyde because he gives Hyde an animal quality. Sort of ape-like, cat-like, I don't know. But I believe him as Hyde.
—J. Lansberg

Favorite mad doctors... How about:
1. Herbert West from the *Re-Animator* movies. He was one crazy and drivin' S.O.B.
2. Dr. Logan from *Day of the Dead*. Come on, he tried to train the living dead and fed them pieces of dead people he saved in a fridge.
3. Dr. Frankenstein from *Young Frankenstein*. I don't think I need to elaborate here.
—Jason

No question—Dr. Paul Carruthers (Bela Lugosi) from *The Devil Bat*. Goggles, shaving lotion, bats, One-Shot McGuire... how can it not make the top five!
—Mike

1. George Zucco in *The Mad Ghoul*. The brilliant mind twisted by love—it's the old bromide, but pulled off in grand style by Zucco who makes poor David Bruce the ultimate dupe to his plans. Science be damned, this guy wants a roll in the hay with Evelyn Ankers, and if a few corpses get mutilated, a few folks get their hearts cut out, that's the price to be paid for love.
2. John Carradine in *Captive Wild Woman*. Unlike brother scientist Zucco, Carradine's only focus is scientific progress. We're still not sure what he's trying to prove with the animal glands. It's a very Dr. Moreau-like process, but there's no doubting John's dedication or insane state of mind. Great stuff.

David Bruce is George Zucco's "ultimate dupe" in *The Mad Ghoul*.

3. Onslow Stevens in *House of Dracula*. Stevens is one of the best noble men of medicine, transformed by a good deed. What scientist could resist finding out what makes Dracula, Larry Talbot and The Frankenstein Monster tick? Unlike Karloff's Dr. Niemann, Dr. Edelmen is a doctor with a sincere desire to help mankind. Of course everything goes wrong—you can't get mixed up with the Universal monsters without paying the price—but this is one of the last great gems of a performance from the classic Universal horror period.
4. Bela Lugosi in *The Return of the Ape Man* and *Bowery at Midnight*. *Return of the Ape Man:* One of Lugosi's straighter performances for Monogram—it doesn't have the goofy energy (or outcome) of *The Ape Man*, but it does

show Bela in a serious mood doing serious (?) work in the old lab. Certainly not as colorful as Mirakle from *Murders in the Rue Morgue* or as gonzo as Dr. Vollin in *The Raven*, but this is a good, solid man-of-science turn for Lugosi in one of the better Monogram/Sam Katzman flicks and deserves some of the recognition other Lugosi movies already enjoy. *Bowery at Midnight*: Rather too similar to *The Human Monster*, this crime/horror flick has a better script and cast than some other Lugosi vehicles, and Wallace Fox punches the thing home. A nice turn from Bela as a doc with a split personality.

5. Boris Karloff in *Frankenstein 1970*. Why in the world *this* movie and *this* performance? Karloff's turns in the Columbia Mad Doctor series are all solid entertainments, *Black Friday* the same. He paid the price for tampering in *The Invisible Ray* and there's nobody as hell-bent on revenge as Dr. Neimann, but Karloff is so over-the-top in this movie, just chewing the scenery to bits, that it amps the enjoyment level of this Howard Koch effort right to the ceiling. He made better movies (lots of 'em) and was better in them, but there's something wonderfully seedy about the movie and Karloff's approach that hits the right Saturday afternoon chord.

And Peter Cushing in *anything*.
—Courtney Joyner

Peter Cushing as the obsessed mad doctor Frankenstein in *The Curse of Frankenstein*

1. Dr. Henry Frankenstein (Colin Clive, 1931/1935, *Frankenstein/Bride of Frankenstein*): What can I say? This guy in the number one spot was an offer I couldn't refuse. Without a doubt, the Godfather of all the movie mad doctors!
2. Dr. Pretorius (Ernest Thesiger, 1935, *Bride of Frankenstein*): Tremendous evil, not to mention that zany haircut and white robe have become the epitome of the mad doctor. Pretorius is second only to Dr. Frankenstein. Just listen to Pretorius while conversing with Clive's Frankenstein... "You think I'm mad. Perhaps I am... Now think, what a world astounding collaboration we should be—you and I together!" He's simply meant to be on this list.
3. Jack Griffin aka the Invisible Man (Claude Rains, 1933, *The Invisible Man*): This was Rains' American film debut, and it came under some trying circumstances. After all, he was totally covered in bandages, and was almost forced completely to act with his voice. "Here we go gathering nuts in May on a cold and frosty morning...."
4. Dr. Bill Cortner (Herb Evers, 1962, *The Brain That Wouldn't Die*): What a romantic mad doctor this guy was. He so loved his fiancée, Jan (played by Virginia Leith) that he kept alive her severed head after she was decapitated in a terrible auto accident. For most of the film, he searches for the perfect body to go with it. Now, if that's not love, I don't know what is?
5. Dr. Gustav Niemann (Boris Karloff, 1944, *House of Frankenstein*): The man who escaped from Neustadt Prison and tried to follow in Henry Frankenstein's footsteps certainly accomplished enough to warrant the number five spot on this list. And it was quite an ironic part with the character filling the mad doctor's shoes, and the actor portraying him being the one who played that mad doctor's famous creation in the first three *Frankenstein* films.
—Sam Borowski

In order of their appearance on the screen, the top five loony docs are, in my opinion:
1. Dr. Bohmer (*Ghost of Frankenstein*, Universal, 1942). As portrayed by Lionel Atwill, Bohmer, the junior partner of Dr. Ludwig Frankenstein, allows professional jealousy to push him over the edge. Thus, he transplants the wily Ygor's brain into the Monster with predictable chaotic consequences.
2. "Temporary Insanity" describes my next favorite mad doctor, Dr. Frank Mannering. Mannering (Patric Knowles)

Colin Clive and Ernest Thesiger play God in *Bride of Frankenstein*.

is a kind, compassionate and quite rational M.D. in *Frankenstein Meets the Wolf Man* (Universal, 1943). Toward the end of the film, he completely looses it in a sudden mad desire to "see the Monster at its full strength." Wildly revving up the power to the Monster's electrodes, only the screaming and pleading of lovely aristocratic Ilsa Frankenstein (Ilona Massey) restores him to his senses before the walls come tumbling down—quite literally.

3. Next, Dr. Andrew Forbes (George Zucco) is the primary care archeologist to a homicidal giant bird in PRC Pictures' *The Flying Serpent* (1946). Dr. Forbes' patient also happens to be an ancient Aztec god named Quetzalcoatl who obligingly zaps those hapless folks who manage to annoy the not-so-good doc.

4. Fast forwarding nine years to Ed Wood's *Bride of the Monster* (1955), Lugosi delivers the ultimate Bela "over the top" performance as Dr. Eric Vornoff. Driven from his homeland by those who, quite naturally, mistook his genius for madness, Bela pulls out all the stops. Only an atomic explosion (yes, an atomic bomb!) puts an end to this mad doctor's practice.

5. My fifth and final favorite mad doctor is Emil Zurich as played by the ever-sinister Henry Daniell in 1959's *Four Skulls of Jonathan Drake* from Vogue Pictures. Dr. Zurich spends his considerable lifetime (200 years) removing and shrinking the heads of the unfortunate male members of the Drake family. Finally, Jonathan Drake figures a way to remove the doctor's shingle… permanently.
—Phil Bisson.

Mad Doctors in Movies:
1. Peter Cushing in Hammer's *Frankenstein* movie series
2. Vincent Price in the two *Dr. Phibes* movies
3. Colin Clive in the first two Universal *Frankenstein* movies
4. Basil Rathbone in *Son of Frankenstein*
5. Kenneth Branagh in *Mary Shelley's Frankenstein*
    (Honorable mention to Fredric March in his Oscar-winning role in *Dr. Jekyll and Mr. Hyde*, Bela Lugosi in *Bride of the Monster* and Jeremy Irons in *Dead Ringers*)

Mad Doctors on Television:
1. Jack Palance as Dr. Jekyll (1969)
2. Harley Quinn (*Batman: The Animated Series* [and *Birds of Prey*])
3. Leonard Whiting as Dr. Frankenstein from *Frankenstein: The True Story* (1973)
4. Dr. Eric Lang (*Dark Shadows*)
5. Paracelsus (*Beauty and the Beast*)
—Jeff Thompson

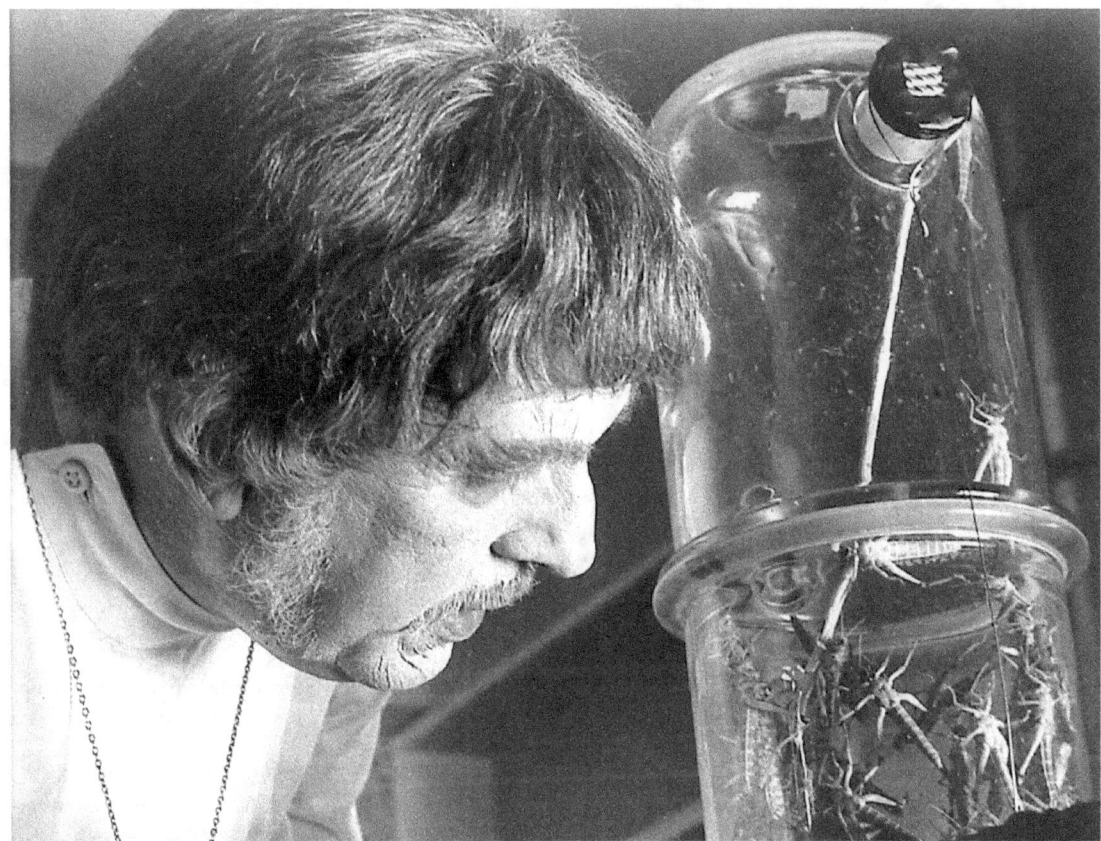

Vincent Price as the "delightfully twisted and ingenious" Dr. Phibes

Five favorite mad doctors:
1. Peter Cushing as Baron Frankenstein in *Frankenstein Must Be Destroyed*—In all six times Cushing played the role, never was he as ruthless or condescending as he was in this film. Like most mad doctors in cinema, he has but one single focus to be carried out despite any obstacles. In this case, to transplant the brain of an insane, dying colleague into another healthy body. Along the way he commits robbery, kidnapping, murder and even rape. Never was the Baron this unsympathetic (or delicious to the audience)!
2. Lionel Atwill as Dr. Rigas in *Man Made Monster*—This was the best of Lionel's mad doctor roles (the film also introduced Lon Chaney, Jr., to the horror genre). Atwill's bug eyes were right up there with the best of them (except for George Zucco). But nobody could match his leer, especially when he forcefully straps Anne Nagel to his lab table, intent on killing her with electricity. All of Atwill's roles were delightful, but here he shines (glows?).
3. As mentioned earlier, the eyes have it—and George Zucco has the eyes! My favorite of his roles is Professor Andoheb in *The Mummy's Hand*, but since that character isn't a mad doctor, I'll select Dr. Morris in *The Mad Ghoul*. Compared to some of his other portrayals, Dr. Morris was rather low-key, but his eyes still reflected the character's evil and lechery (lusting after Evelyn Ankers, despite her atrocious 1940s hairstyle)!
4. Jeffery Combs as Herbert West in *Re-Animator*—Herbert West is a great character: intense, pouting, sullen, surly, sardonic and brilliant. He is so enamored of his glow-in-the-dark re-agent that he fails to see its results. Every person or animal he brings back to life is outraged, murderous and destructive. West is oblivious to this unless he's defending himself from one of these corpses. He even ignores a naked Barbara Crampton.
5. Bela Lugosi as Dr. Vollin in *The Raven*—You really have to admire a guy who builds his own torture chamber and talks to a stuffed raven and bust of Pallas, spouting lines like "Poe, you are avenged!" (I didn't know Poe needed avenging.) Bela is cultured and maniacal. When he laughs at his prisoner Boris Karloff, he is *way* over the top. This is one of Bela's better roles and the one time he should have received top billing over Karloff.
—Gary Billings

1. Dr. Phibes—First of all, it's Vincent Price. Ya can't go wrong there. And second, ol' Phibesy was just so delightfully twisted and ingenious. All those clever ways to send his victims screaming to their graves. I could never wait to see his next little gimmick. Yeah, I gotta vote for ol' Doc Phibes, for sure.
2. Dr. Plato Zorba (from *13 Ghosts*)—While he may not be considered by some to be a mad scientist (since in the original—and best—movie, he was already dead), you

5. Dr. Henry Jekyll—Now this guy knew how to party! He creates a lively brew that brings out the animal in himself and then he goes and has his way with the ladies! He may be butt ugly, but he certainly woos the frillies off them, doesn't he? You just have to admire a guy who creates juice that can make him a dashing lover even if he has a face only a nearsighted mom could love. He may have been mad, but he definitely had some ideas of what's fun! He gets *my* vote!

6. Any mad scientist played by King Karloff! That says it all. If he were a mad scientist in a movie, that performance became a favorite of mine. Karloff was, is and always will be the king of the monsters and madmen! Long may he rest in peace, although he shall never be forgotten! Any scientist he played could both charm and give you the willies, all at the same time. Sorry to be vague on this one, but so it goes. Karloff made the role, not the other way around.
—Tom Detoro (aka "Renfield")

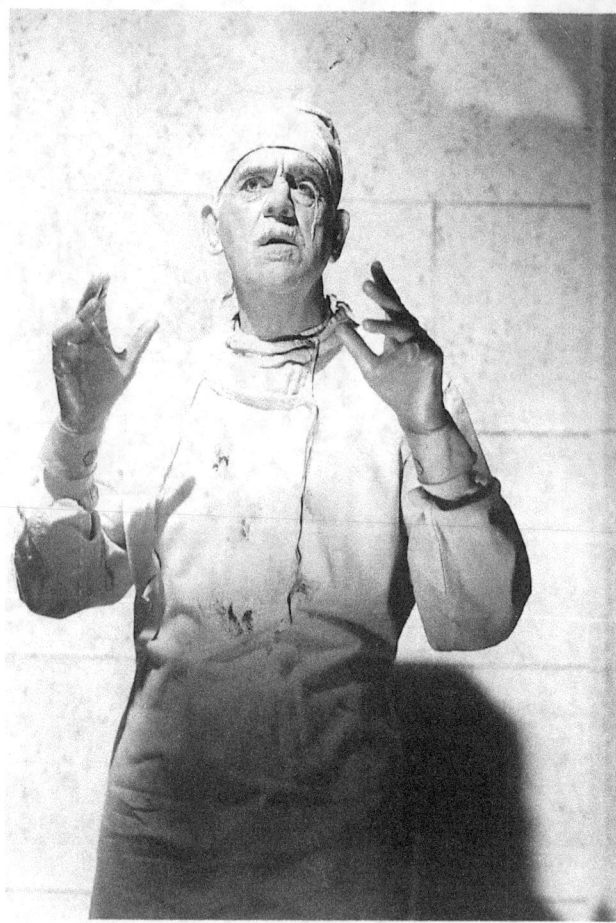

"Karloff was, is and always will be the king of the monsters and madmen!... and mad doctors." *Frankenstein 1970*

have to consider him for a spot here. I mean, how cool is it to hunt ghosts.... and even *capture* them. And then live right there in the same house with the spooks you captured?!! I mean, wouldn't you think they'd be sore at you?! Yeah, he had to be nuts, all right. But ya gotta admire anyone who hunts ghosts for giggles, no? So dead or not, I gotta vote for Doc Zorba as a favorite whacked out scientist, even though I'm pretty sure not many will agree with me.

3. Herbert West—Oh, okay, so he's not one of the "oldies but goodies." He's still a Class-A psycho. Anyone who re-animates dead folks for fun is okay in my book. And he was always so deadpan serious about it! A delightfully delusional mad scientist. He's on *my* list.

4. Dr. Henry Frankenstein—In *any* incarnation, this guy has got to be on the list. No other mad scientist has popped up in the annals of horror as often as crazy Henry/Victor/The Baron. No matter who plays him, he'll always be way up there on the nutso scale. I mean, c'mon.... sewing parts of cadavers together and then using the ol' key on the kite trick to zap 'em to life? Wow. Yeah, he's mad as a hatter, all right.... and totally oblivious to the fact! Dr. Frankenstein goes on my list, too.

The mad doctors in my life are:
1. Dr. Frankenstein (Colin Clive)—Power obsessed. Playing God. Skulking through cemeteries.
2. Dr. Pretorius (Ernest Thesiger)—Out of his mind, not to mention he has that small, coffin-looking box full of miniature people.
3. Dr. Moreau (Charles Laughton)—He scared me to death… everyone scared me to death in this! Yet I'm still alive! I'm now the undead… good gosh! The House of Pain!
4. Baron Frank (Boris Karloff)—*Frankenstein 1970*. First Frankenstein movie I saw. I couldn't speak English yet, but was enthralled by Boris' voice! I would watch anything with him in it! In *Frankenstein 1970* his creation was creepy since it was all bandaged up!
5. Dr. Gogol (Peter Lorre)—from *Mad Love*. He's obsessed!! "But I *must* have you!" Mad doctors are the scariest, because they take their time.
—Rose Solar

While it is difficult narrowing down a list to a top five from some many fine contenders, here is my top five list of the Greatest Mad Scientists of All Time:
1. Dr. Victor Frankenstein (Peter Cushing), whose series of movies still remains one of the finest horror series of all time. While the Byronic qualities remain essentially the same throughout the series, Cushing's Frankenstein does range from being fairly benign (in *Evil of Frankenstein*) to egregiously malignant (in *Frankenstein Must Be Destroyed*). Cushing's portrayal of world-weary doggedness in pursuit of his goal remains memorable, though ironically, it is his assistant in *Revenge of Frankenstein* who achieves the greatest success in his experiments.

2. Dr. Henry Frankenstein (Colin Clive) is still one of the screen's most memorable dreamers. His seems a fevered and tormented soul, despite his exaltation of knowing what it feels like to be God. Sadly, he never takes responsibility for his neglect of his creation, but it is hard to beat the one-two punch of *Frankenstein* and *Bride of Frankenstein*.

3. Dr. Bernardo (John Carradine) from *Everything You Wanted to Know About Sex But Were Afraid to Ask* remains one of the maddest mad scientists of all-time. Carradine was good at playing crazy medicos, but this Woody Allen-written send-up of the genre allows him to be totally unfettered and extremely funny. (Bernardo wants to create, for example, the world's largest diaphragm, to force a man to have sex with a large loaf of bread, to measure the pulse rate of a woman being gang-banged by cub scouts. Masters and Johnson, eat your heart out).

4. Dr. Janos Rukh (Boris Karloff) from *The Invisible Ray* belongs up there. Karloff creates a character that is far better off in the laboratory than he is in dealing with people. Karloff limned many fine medical luminaries, but to me, Rukh is one of his most memorable, with the added bonus of his pairing with Bela.

5. Dr. Gogol (Peter Lorre) from *Mad Love* makes the final cut, beating out Lorre's amusing turns as Dr. Einstein, Dr. Lorantz and Dr. Adolphus Bedlo. Lorre's acting as Gogol isn't as caricatured as some of his later work, and it is a dazzling piece of acting. With eye movements and body language, Lorre conveys Gogol's obsession: love, frustration, exhaustion, madness and torment. This is one of horror's greatest *tour de force* performances, well worth savoring for Lorre's ability to create sympathy for a vindictive, bug-eyed creep.

—Dennis Fischer

"Michael Gough is the arrogantly prissy doctor who smirks most cowardly in his embrace of Konga."

My Five Ghastly Mad Scientists (And Five Runners-up):

1. John Dehner's decidedly loopy departure from slick-tongued villains, and instead he plays it strictly for shtick in *The Bowery Boys Meet the Monsters* (1954).
2. Narda Onyz is the sensually ripe over-the-top relative of Herr Frankenstein in *Jesse James Meets Frankenstein's Daughter* (1966).
3. Whit Bissell becomes the self-concerned dedicated scientist off his collective rocker in *I Was a Teenage Frankenstein* (1957).
4. Donald Murphy plays the smooth, venomous, handsome and classy do-it-his-way-or-no-way murderous scientist in *Frankenstein's Daughter* (1958).
5. John Hoyt as the pitiless live puppet master scientist, from *Attack of the Puppet People* (1958), who is god of his own cruel laboratory world, definitely one brick shy of a load here.
6. Robert Evans is purely vicious as the evil, twisted psycho maniac in *The Fiend Who Walked the West* (1958). He does snivel when justice turns the tables.
7. Michael Gough as the arrogantly prissy doctor who smirks most cowardly in his embrace of *Konga* (1961) at the finale.
8. Guy Rolfe's former haughty in-charge dominance is broken down, then sheer panic results from Oscar Homolka's torturous lies at the end of *Mr. Sardonicus* (1961).
9. Torin Thatcher's sadistic streak is turned to pure jelly as his sorcerer's bag of tricks won't save his bacon when he's on the receiving end of fear, horror and death from *The Seventh Voyage of Sinbad* (1958).
10. Niall MacGinnis' cunningly crafty portrayal of evil starts to crumble when the tables are turned and the parchment is passed to him. He does a great warlock sprint and dash to try to save his skin in true sniveler's fashion in *Curse of the Demon* (1957).

—William Wilkerson

Peter Cushing's portrayal of the Baron is the most complex and consistently developed mad scientist in the movies.

1. Peter Cushing's performance as Baron Frankenstein from the Hammer Frankenstein series—The Hammer Frankenstein series reveals Peter Cushing's portrayal of the Baron to be the most complex and consistently developed mad scientist in movies. When looked at consecutively, we have the evil obsession of *Curse of Frankenstein*, the in-disguise dedicated man of medicine in *Revenge of Frankenstein*, the emerging cynic of *Evil of Frankenstein*, the dashing romantic rogue of *Frankenstein Created Woman*, the almost bitter misanthrope of *Frankenstein Must Be Destroyed* and the aging and pathetic world-weary medical adventurer of *Frankenstein and the Monster from Hell*. Cushing has created a richness of character that is multi-layered, creating one of the most memorable horror film performances yet created.

2. Colin Clive's Dr. Frankenstein in *Frankenstein* and *Bride of Frankenstein*—Colin Clive's version of Dr. Frankenstein is more high-strung than Cushing's and also more one-dimensional, but Clive's obsession set the standards for other mad scientists to come. His wild-eyed cries of "It's alive" as he looks skyward, ranting and mumbling to himself, or his rude welcoming of human visitors to his secret watchtower, including his bride-to-be, only demonstrates his fatalistic dedication to the world of science, daring to rob heaven of its secrets at any cost.

3. Pierre Brasseur as Dr. Genessiere in *Eyes Without a Face* (1960)—This haunting French horror thriller still mesmerizes with its rich black-and-white photography and fairy tale quality. We have a disfigured Edith Scob, wearing an ivory-white mask, literally floating around the mansion and nearby forest, as her obsessed and guilt-ridden doctor/father abducts young female victims, murders them and removes their faces in gruesome operations, attempting to restore his daughter's ravished features. Brasseur's performance is quietly evil—his non-expressive face and delicate way with his daughter contrasts to his perverse stalking of innocent young women—making him one of the more subtle mad scientists of movies.

4. Lionel Atwill in *Doctor X, Mystery of the Wax Museum, Murders in the Zoo* and *The Vampire Bat*—The bulky and steely-eyed Lionel Atwill, sometimes wearing thick glasses and maintaining a stoic face reinforced by a formal British voice, seems to be playing against type when he becomes one of the first actors to be stereotyped as a mad scientist (even becoming a red herring in *Doctor X*). Atwill's insanity, emerging at some pivotal point during each production, always seems to be revealed shockingly with the maximum of surprise, as his proper Brit persona is revealed to harbor raving passions just beneath the surface that seem to burst forth from him much as lava overflows an erupting volcano.

5. Bela Lugosi in *The Devil Bat, The Invisible Ghost, Return of the Apeman, Bride of the Monster*, etc.—Bela Lugosi, the best mad doctor of poverty row Hollywood, is so successful because of his unwavering dedication to his performance, even when cardboard sets ripple around him and the most unspecial effects threaten to sink any credibility the movie might possess. Supporting actors might seem stiff or over-emote, but the consummate professional Lugosi never delivers less than his best. And his megalomaniacal leanings often become the only reason to keep watching.

—Gary J. Svehla

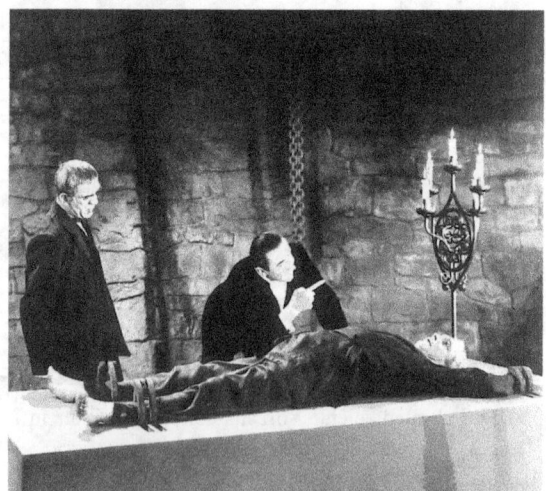

Bela Lugosi was the best mad doctor on Poverty Row. Above: Boris and Bela in *The Raven*

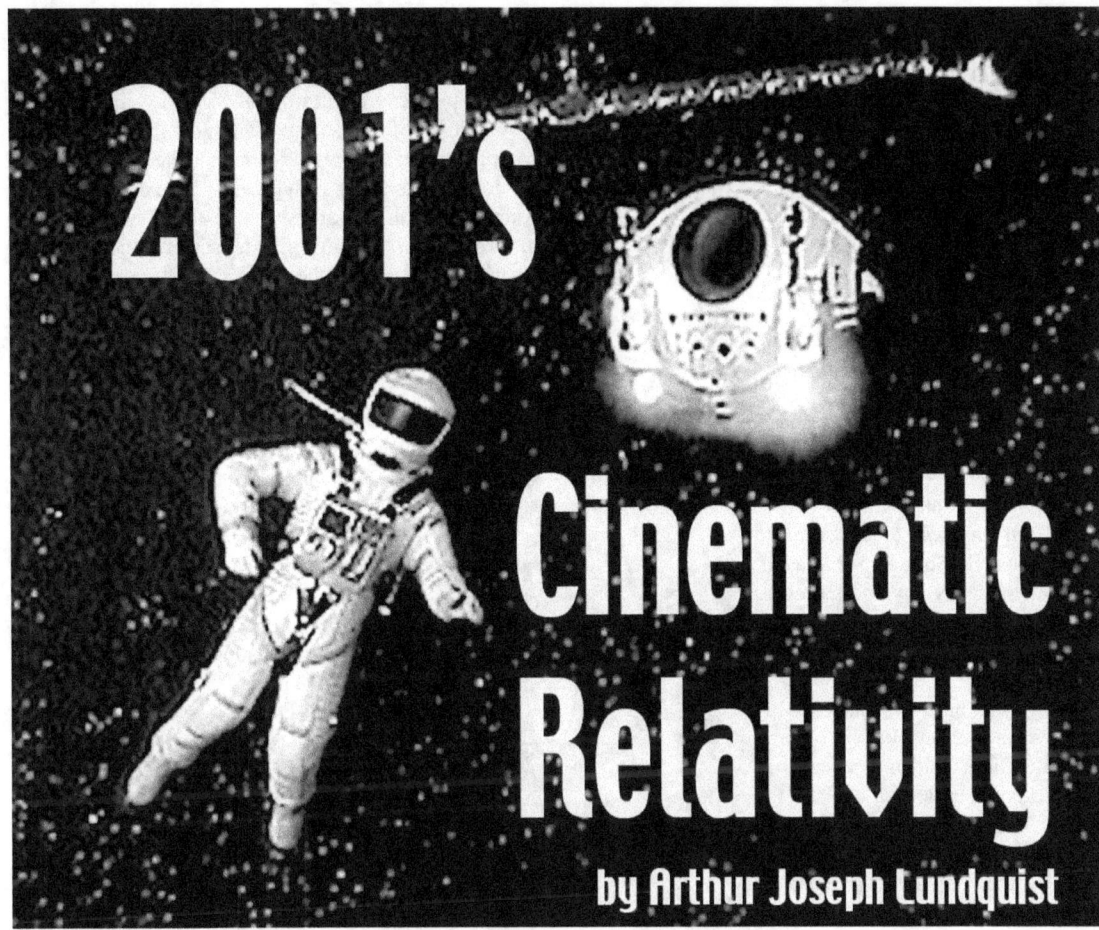

2001's Cinematic Relativity

by Arthur Joseph Lundquist

If in 1968 there was an image the world had never seen before, an image for which the world was ready, it was the sight of the Earth, tiny, alone and vulnerable, floating into view from the other side of the Moon. When that image was seen in all its glory in the opening moments of *2001: A Space Odyssey*, with the beckoning sun onscreen and the exultant music of Richard Strauss filling the theater, audiences erupted into applause.

Only months before, *Planet of the Apes* had fulfilled that impossible dream of sci-fi freaks, a science fiction film that everybody wanted to see. Who could have dared dream of what followed in April 1968: a science fiction film that was one of the acknowledged greatest movies of all times.

And yet, *2001: A Space Odyssey* was not quite the vindication we fans had waited for. It seemed to have absolutely come out of nowhere, owing nothing to just about any sci-fi flick ever made. It sounded different. Its performances were different. The way you watched it was different. It looked so real that you could absolutely believe in every frame.

It is amazing now to look back at the most ambitious speculative films to come out of Hollywood before *2001* and see special effects that just cry out "Fake! Fake!" Look at *The Conquest of Space* and see the shimmer on the side of its obviously formed plastic space station. See the thick blue matte lines surrounding the burning Sphinx of the Morlocks in *The Time Machine*. Eyeball the truly pathetic ape costumes in *One Million Years B.C.* Wince at the flying police hanging on wires in front of a back projection screen in *Fahrenheit 451*. Japanese and Italian filmmakers could ask audiences to accept the artificiality as part of their style, but how many adult American moviegoers would?

2001 didn't justify genre movies—it made them seem pathetically inadequate. *War of the Worlds*? *This Island Earth*? *Forbidden Planet*? *Robinson Crusoe on Mars*? By comparison, what American space movie *didn't* look like it was made for children? What mainstream genre movie actually seemed to be *about* something (other than explosions)? *Fantastic Voyage*? *Crack in the World*? *One Million Years B.C.*? It was enough to make you ashamed of all the movies you used to love.

And yet, as I sit down to write this, not altogether intentionally, on January 1, 2001, I wonder. I have always been struck by the way one of Stanley Kubrick's most celebrated set pieces, Slim Pickens riding a thermonuclear weapon to Armageddon in *Dr. Strangelove*, resembles a crashing nuclear bomber in the 1957 B-movie *Kronos*.

The Creeping Unknown's astronauts created the illusion of weightlessness during their doomed flight.

"space ship" is floored with wooden duckboards, but there is one moment when we see an astronaut walk up the circular wall of his space ship, and for that moment the film perfectly creates the illusion of weightlessness. It was done, of course, by building a set that could be completely rotated with the camera locked in place while the actor walks along with gravity. This echoes in *2001* when a Pan Am stewardess walks all the way up a wall in zero gravity, and, on a grander scale, in the incredible centrifuge interiors of the space ship Discovery (though I'm perfectly willing to believe a more likely inspiration was Fred Astaire dancing on the ceiling in 1951's *Royal Wedding*).

Kubrick's special effects are presented to us in long takes, without dialogue or plot business while we watch and savor their realism, much as the magic tricks used as special effects in *The Time Travelers* had been presented. The device doesn't really work in *The Time Travelers*, but its presentation of tricks in real time reality may have been a spur to *2001*.

And how a German scientist in *The First Man into Space* (1958) seems to foreshadow Dr. Strangelove himself. Or how the teddy boys of *These Are The Damned* suggest the droogs of *A Clockwork Orange*. Maybe Kubrick or Clarke or Doug Trumbull *did* spend some time watching cheap B-movies. And maybe some dumb monster flicks hold a few seeds to Kubrick's masterwork.

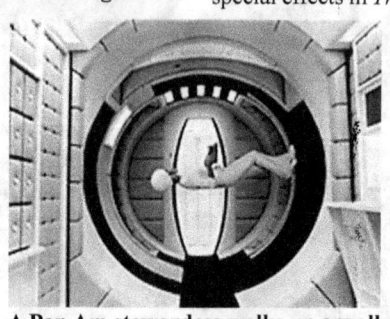

A Pan Am stewardess walks up a wall in *2001*.

Surprisingly, in the 1950s, the most realistic space movie effects came from a TV cartoon. On Walt Disney's *Disneyland* series, sandwiched among the likes of *Johnny Tremain* and *Davy Crockett*, were a series of specials examining the future of space exploration. One of them, "Mars and Beyond," is highlighted by a trip to Mars, using cartoon animation. This sequence is very impressive. The space craft, painted on celluloid then photographed on an animation stand, moves across the screen with a smoothness and reality of motion somehow more "realistic" and convincing to the eye than the miniature space craft used in *Forbidden Planet* or *The Conquest of Space* or any live action movie until then. Douglas Trumbull's crew for *2001* adapted the technique by placing still photographs of miniature space crafts on an animation stand and animating them like painted cells. The effect is almost hypnotic. This idea was taken a generation forward with *2001*'s use, for the first time, of 3-dimensional models and cameras mounted on computer-controlled animated stands. (More about "Mars and Beyond" later.)

Admittedly, it's pretty hard to imagine the cultivated Mr. Kubrick sitting through *Angry Red Planet*. Hard to imagine him not gritting his teeth at its B-movie dialogue, groaning at the Hollywood jungle set that represents the planet Mars. And yet, could Kubrick have *missed* the one thing here that is extraordinary? The scenes that take place on the surface of Mars were filmed by printing a black-and-white negative of the scene (with much of its detail removed by acid) on top of a positive, tinted red. The *intention* of director Ib Melchoir and his collaborators was to replace areas of detail on the photographic image with flat areas of a single color, so that footage of the actors would blend believably with comic-book-style drawings of Mars (they didn't have the money for complex matte paintings). The unexpected *result* was to evoke a truly alien world by changing cinematic reality, the photographic emulsion itself. It almost works, and might have been the starting point for some of the truly unearthly landscapes we see during *2001*'s flight through the Star Gate.

An animated scene from Disney's "Mars and Beyond"

In the middle of the monster movie *The Creeping Unknown*, we watch some astronauts on the first trip into space. Their "space suits" resemble medieval armor, the

In *The Thing From Another World* a group of Arctic explorers fan out on the ice to determine the shape of a buried spacecraft. The moment reaches its weird climax as they realize the object makes a perfect circle. The moment is almost primordially impressive, and I think, echoes in *2001* when both its ape men at the dawn of time and its space explorers on the Moon confront for the first time a black monolith from space, and in both

The Arctic explorers spread out on the ice to determine the shape of the buried ship in *The Thing*.

The astronauts surround the monolith in *2001*.

instances the first thing they do is to almost instinctually fan out into a circle around it. In Kubrick's film the moment takes on an almost religious significance.

One of *2001*'s most original and influential ideas was its soundtrack of recognizable classical music. Kubrick's official explanation is that he had engaged in the common practice of scoring his rough cut with classical music as a guide for composer Alex North, but as time went on, became so enamored of the mythic associations evoked by Strauss and Khatchaturian that all of North's music ended up on the cutting room floor. Great story. Probably true. But *maybe* somebody remembered the snatches of Borodin that score *Fire Maidens of Outer Space*, the music from Gustav Holst's "The Planets" (to this day, one of the most influential pieces of science fiction music) used in the original BBC TV serial *The Quatermass Experiment* and the American TV series *Tales of Tomorrow* (along with other classical composers), and don't even get me started on the use of "Les Preludes" in the *Flash Gordon* serials.

Most of the effects in the Russian space film *Planeta Berg* (*Planet of Storms*, 1962) are fairly routine, although well rendered by 1960s American standards. But watch out for one moment when a female cosmonaut joyfully floats about her orbiting spacecraft. We can see her entire body, with no wires or supports visible anywhere around her. However, the alert eye may notice an open airlock door directly behind her. This is the first time I can remember seeing a film create the illusion of weightlessness by the technique that *2001* would make the industry standard: suspending an actor from a wire directly over the camera, with the camera shooting straight up so the wires are concealed by the actor's own body.

I believe *Planeta Berg*'s influence went beyond special effects. In one scene the cosmonauts discover evidence of human habitation on a Venus that is otherwise like Earth in the time of the dinosaurs. They speculate among themselves:

Vershinin: Suppose civilized beings had flown here and remained for some unknown reason and lost contact with their own planet. In an alien atmosphere and conditions they...
Boborov: ...would perish.
Vershinin: Some would survive, but go wild in the brutal fight for survival and adjustment to local conditions. No time for culture in that case. Only the strong would survive.
Alyosha: And savages would appear among the dinosaurs...
Vershinin: Before the local apes...
Alyosha: ...appeared and the future master of the planet began to evolve.

The Russian spaceship in *Planeta Berg*

Later there is speculation that Venus and perhaps even Earth might have been settled in prehistoric times by beings from Mars. One can easily imagine Kubrick and Clarke in a coffee shop, after the flick, knocking these concepts back and forth, tweaking them here and there to make them a little more logical, a little more interesting, a little more like the final premise of *2001*.

Of course, these were fairly common ideas in written science fiction. Arthur C. Clarke didn't need a movie to find them. However, another moment in *Planeta Berg* comes much closer to home. When two cosmonauts are trapped by a lava flow, they climb on the shoulders of their humanoid robot and instruct it to carry them to safety. Half way across the lava, the robot reports: "Further movement with a load endangers my mechanism." One cosmonaut orders the other: "Turn off the self-protection, open the door, panel 5," to switch

The desperate astronauts must ride the robot across a lava flow in *Planeta Berg*.

The astronauts must find a way to destroy Hal in *2001*.

personality disintegrate. If this is truly an influence, in every instance Kubrick and Clarke have made choices that illuminate human possibilities barely suggested in *Planeta Berg*.

I can't imagine Kubrick *not* sitting down to watch *Destination Moon*. Because of its technical polish and script by Robert Heinlein, for decades it was the one sci-fi flick that writers and keen fans of written science fiction would admit liking. Unfortunately, by the mid-1960s, virtually every aspect of the film reeked with old-movie phoniness, from its mechanic's Brooklyn accent to the moment when the head scientist bids farewell on the launch pad to his wife, played by an actress with obviously no idea what she's doing there. Every bid to raise our sympathy feels forced, every piece of comic relief sounds contemptibly stupid.

Yet, if you can ignore the dialogue, there is something genuinely powerful about the film, about its commitment to present a voyage to the Moon with as much fidelity to scientific accuracy as was humanly possible in 1950, which translates into a faith and wonder in the ability of the human race to transcend their own world, given the will to do so.

I think Kubrick takes that from *Destination Moon*, and strips away everything else. Gone is the ticking clock. Gone are the personal conflicts, the dramatic confrontations, and the overt comic relief. *2001*'s

off the robot's programming without interfering with its ability to function. Before they can, the robot announces: "I'm compelled to get rid of the load," and prepares to toss them into the lava. The desperate men start pulling wires and hammering its inner mechanism, accidentally causing the robot's sound system to play an incredibly inappropriate recording of 1940s big band music. (Those of you who saw *Planeta Berg* under one of its Roger Corman re-edits [see *Voyage to the Planet of Prehistoric Women*], most of this was lost in the dubbing.)

This sounds to me like the conception of the most emotionally wrenching sequence in *2001*. Instead of a cosmonaut switching off an emotionless machine, *2001* gives us an astronaut lobotomizing the one truly human character in the film, the computer HAL. Instead of big band music, *2001*'s HAL sings "Daisy," a song evocative of the age when travel meant bicycles and buggies. And instead of the robot's quick systems crash, HAL's voice slows down and down as we watch his

Kubrick forces the audience to look for signs of humanity in *2001*.

people casually exchange dialogue filled with everyday banalities, mentioning enough family names and issues to give you a feeling of life outside of the movie frame, but the film does not try to invest your emotions in them on the typical dramatic level.

Yet *2001: A Space Odyssey* does have much to involve the mind and the heart. Given that its characters generate so little human interest, Kubrick forces the audience to look for signs of humanity in the wideness of the Cinerama screen, in the space surrounding the performers, in the stretches of time surrounding every line of dialogue. We glimpse it in the food the astronauts eat, in the exercises and zero-gravity toilets that must sustain human life in outer space. Through these details the film builds a picture of the tininess and fragility of human life, and a genuine awe at the effort and ambition it takes to send human beings to the stars.

I remember in particular a scene in *2001* when astronaut Frank Poole (Gary Lockwood), on the first manned mission to Jupiter, sits on a sunbath table watching videotape on which his parents wish him a happy birthday. He cannot speak to them directly, due to the seven minutes it takes radio waves to reach the space ship Discovery. Listening to his parents babble about personal trivia, he seems achingly far from home, his birthday itself seemingly meaningless, so far out of Earth orbit. Lying there, wearing white shorts, white shoes and socks, and a pair of sunglasses, Poole seems like some half-formed embryo, fragile and naked, ridiculously unsuited to such a hostile environment. In that moment, after a lifetime of taking space travel for granted, I was suddenly awed by what a revolutionary concept it is to send human beings into space.

This moment seems to me to be a perfect visual distillation of an exchange from the climax of the 1936 H.G. Wells/Menzies/Korda epic *Things to Come*. As two men of the year 2036 look up at the sky, they talk about humanity's future among the stars.

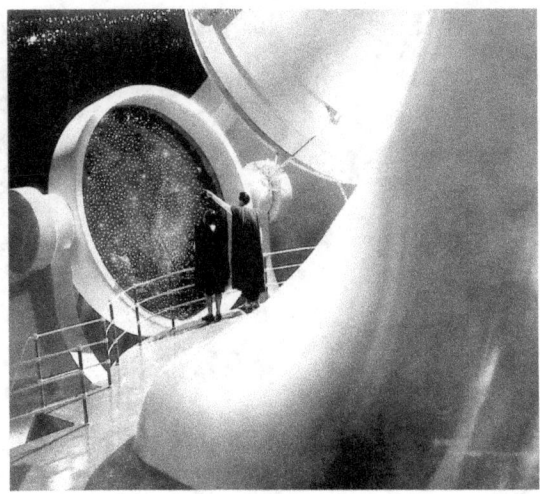

Stanley Kubrick was not impressed with the classic *Things to Come*.

Caba: And when he has conquered all the deeps of space and all the mysteries of time—still he will be beginning.
Passworthy: But we're such little creatures. Poor humanity, so fragile, so weak—little... little animals.
Cabal: Little animals.

We know that Kubrick saw *Things to Come*. We even know the day, thanks to the December 10, 1964, entry in Clarke's diary: "Stanley calls after screening H.G. Wells' *Things to Come*, and says he'll *never* see another movie I recommend." Alas, we have no record of just what Kubrick didn't like. It may have been Wells' way of directly lecturing us on his film's message, which Kubrick never does. Indeed, in *2001* Kubrick strips away so much exposition that the viewer may have no idea what is going on the first time round.

Still, there is something about the five-act structure of *Things to Come*, which takes off in a long, wordless sequence wherein the debris of a world war is built into a super-city of the future. As rubble is cleared while more and more gigantic machines rise around us, it kind of liberates the imagination and prepares us to accept Wells' super-scientific future.

The spaceship from "Mars and Beyond"

The Disney "Mars and Beyond" special (co-written and directed by Ward Kimball) uses a similarly mind-expanding structure. Broadcast, with a certain mythic resonance, on the day after Christmas 1957, "Mars and

The giant mother ship taking off for the stars in *Close Encounters of the Third Kind* was probably influenced by *2001* as well as "Mars and Beyond."

Beyond" begins with historic speculations about life on Mars, since the time of Plato, including some comical (and highly inaccurate) illustrations of Edgar Rice Burroughs and H.G. Wells. Once having hooked our interest with whimsy, the film then engages our belief with a state-of-the-science examination of the creation and evolution of life on Earth. Concentrating on Mars, the film dazzles us with facts about the Martian environment, and then takes off with the finest 1957 scientific speculation about what forms of alien life may wait there. From moment to moment its speculations get more and more far out, the alien life forms becoming more and more alien until at last they become absolutely abstract, many of them looking like frames from *2001*'s Star Gate. The film ends with an enormous spacecraft taking off for the stars, an image, which I'd wager, percolated in many imaginations over the years to appear (among other places) as the mother ship in *Close Encounters of the Third Kind*.

Perhaps these last two films are among the many that echo in what is, for most people, the most impressive sequence in *2001*, the trip through the Star Gate. Back in those days, everyone I knew simply referred to it as "The Trip." As we are carried, via some of the most hallucinogenic special effects ever seen, down an endless corridor of light, punctuated by freeze-frame reaction shots of Kier Dullea (perhaps inspired by those frozen shots of Tippi Heddren during the exploding gas station sequence in *The Birds*?), through swirling images of galaxies and nebulae (from "Mars and Beyond"?), past unfathomable alien devices (an echo of Expo 67's Gyrotron?) and on through totally alien landscapes blazing with unknown energy (*The Angry Red Planet*? the Cinerama feature *Seven Wonders of the World*?), we are carried out from our every human frame of reference to accept a world where science is indistinguishable from magic, and time seems to have no meaning (influenced by a similarly timeless sequence in *The Graduate* the previous year?).

Mind you, not all of *2001* comes from such base sources. *2001* began with one of the defining images of the Age of Aquarius. It ends with another.

In a scene being duplicated by families around the world, I remember my family sitting in our living room, pouring over a 16-page photo essay in the April 30, 1965, issue of *Life* magazine. Here were the results of photographer Lennart Nilsson's multi-year effort to use microphotography to trace the development of the human fetus. As we saw these images for the first time, they were not tired photographs out of high school health texts, or propaganda brandished by screaming mobs in front of abortion clinics. At that first sight, beholding all of ourselves in a miraculous moment of eternity, there was room for only wonder.

At 11 weeks, a recognizable human child lies surrounded in a round placenta, itself floating in a black void dotted with white specks that resemble stars. In the final picture, at 28 weeks, a fully developed child on the verge of viability, separated from the surrounding blackness by a thin veil of membrane, seems to look back at the reader, to contemplate us from the other side of existence.

To end *2001*, Kubrick brings that image face to face with the other great image of 1968, the lone, fragile Earth as seen from space.

To end *2001*, Kubrick brings that image face to face with the other great image of 1968, the lone, fragile Earth as seen from space. Watching that conclusion today, we behold ourselves as we were in the age of Apollo, children of Earth staring back at our place among the stars, awed with where we have been and the possibilities beyond.

The Trip from *2001* will prove a lasting legacy in sci-fi films.

Post-Script: The Legacy of *2001*

Of course, speculating on what films may have influenced *2001* is only a game. There is, however, no mistaking the influence *2001* wielded in the years that

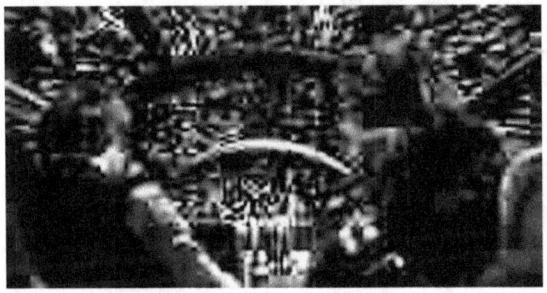

A jump to hyper space in *Star Wars*

followed. Indeed, for nine years *2001: A Space Odyssey* pretty much defined what a science fiction movie was going to be.

After *2001*, special effects were to be watched and savored at length, slowing *Marooned* and *Journey to the Far Side of the Sun* and *Earth II* down to a crawl as space craft move through starry skies, their astronauts floating in zero g, at a length that would have been unimaginable before 1968. Post-Kubrick science fiction movies would be a visual experience, with long, wordless sequences in *Phase IV*, *Silent Running*, *Solaris* and *The Man Who Fell to Earth*. Even an action film like *Rollerball* would reduce its star James Caan to almost wordless imbecility.

2001 was a box office hit without a single major star, a course followed for a very brief moment by *Colossus The Forbin Project*, *The Andromeda Strain*, *THX-1138* and *Silent Running*.

The classical music soundtrack, so radical in 1968, became, after *The Gladiators*, *Zardoz* and *Rollerball*, almost a cliché, one even satirized by the country-western music in *Dark Star*. As late as 1976, John Williams had to talk George Lucas out of filling *Star Wars* with bits of Holst and Liszt and Wagner.

The idea that science fiction should touch on some kind of absolutely cosmic truth, and if you could not actually verbalize what that truth was, so much the better. *The Last Days of Man on Earth. Phase IV. Zardoz. The Man Who Fell to Earth.*

The mind-blowing "Trip" through the Star Gate. How many sci-fi films tried to find some way to crowd

After *2001*, special effects were to be watched and savored at length.

in a psychedelic special effects sequence? The dream sequence in *Journey to the Far Side of the Sun*. *Silent Running*'s flight through Saturn's rings. The moment of conception in *Demon Seed*. The journey into *The Black Hole*. The Trip's most lasting legacy will probably continue to be the jumps to light speed in *Dark Star*, *Star Wars*, *Star Trek: The Motion Picture* and all their descendants and imitations. Not to mention *Star Gate* and its TV spin-off.

Now, I wouldn't want you to think that all this influence by *2001* was necessarily a good thing. Maybe a quicker pace could have saved *Marooned*. Maybe the end of *Phase IV* would make sense with a few words of exposition. Maybe *The Man Who Fell to Earth* would have been more fun had it been a little less meaningful. Perhaps *Silent Running* would be remembered today if it had starred Robert Redford. Maybe *Blade Runner* would mean something if it had concentrated as much on ideas as production design.

After *2001*, any film lacking the budget for seamless, photographically perfect visual effects was going to

Barbara Bain and Martin Landau in *Space 1999*

look "fake," as Ray Harryhausen found when audiences rejected his masterpiece of animation, *Valley of Gwangi*. This was another nail in the coffin of Japanese monster movies, and those who ignored this lesson did so at their peril (see *Logan's Run*).

Probably the single hugest accumulation of all the negative influences of *2001* can be found in the Sylvia and Gerry Anderson TV series *Space: 1999*. Its interior sets of spacecraft and moon bases had that perfect glossy NASA look, with miniatures more realistic than anything seen on television. Often episodes would wordlessly open with spacecraft moving against starscapes backed by classical-sounding music, and end with ominous, cosmically important statements. Yet, the show was at spirit an action-adventure series, and the attempt to emulate *2001* would be positively lethal. Whole episodes grind by at the pace of a snail, and those endings would just leave audiences scratching their head. The quintessential *Space: 1999* episode, "The Black Sun," ends with my personal favorite ersatz Trip, an economical light show featuring people growing old while portentously announcing, "Of course, it's possible that we don't exist." Maybe *Space: 1999* would have been a happier series had it come out in the wake of *Star Wars*.

Ah well. Strange that in the year of its setting, *2001* has been marked by a lack of interest on the part of MGM/UA to re-release the film in the United States. It shuttled through a few minor theaters in the central U.S., and only in the last two weeks of December did it finally begin to play in New York, and if I can, I'm going to go see it again tomorrow. As I sit down to write these words, altogether intentionally, on December 31, 2001, I hope that its title will not make it a thing of the past, that *2001: A Space Odyssey* will remain forever a beacon to all of our tomorrows.

CREDITS:
Director, Producer, Special Photographic Effects Designed and Directed by: Stanley Kubrick; Screenplay: Kubrick & Arthur C. Clarke; Director Of Photography: Geoffrey Unsworth; Additional Photography: John Alcott; Music: Aram Khatchaturian ("Gayane Ballet Suite"); György Ligeti ("Atmospheres," "Lux Aeterna," "Requiem"); Johann Strauss ("The Blue Danube"); Richard Strauss ("Thus Spake Zarathustra"); Special Photographic

Michael York and Jenny Agutter in *Logan's Run*

Effects Supervisors: Wally Veevers, Douglas Trumbull, Con Pederson, Tom Howard; Production Design: Tony Masters, Harry Lange, Ernest Archer; Editor: Ray Lovejoy; Wardrobe: Hardy Amies; Special Photographic Effects Unit: Colin Cantwell, Bruce Logan, Bryan Loftus, David Osborne, Frederick Martin, John Jack Malick; Art Director: John Hoesli; Makeup Artist: Stuart Freeborn

Presented by Metro-Goldwyn-Mayer; 139 minutes (156 at the premiere); Filmed in Super Panavision; released in Cinerama; In Technicolor and Metrocolor

CAST:
Keir Dullea (Dave Bowman); Gary Lockwood (Frank Poole); William Sylvester (Dr. Heywood Floyd); Daniel Richter (Moonwatcher, unnamed in film); Leonard Rossiter (Dr. Andre Smyslov); Margaret Tyzack (Elena); Robert Beatty (Dr. Halvorsen); Sean Sullivan (Dr. Michaels); Douglas Rain (the voice of HAL); Alan Gifford (Poole's dad); Ann Gillis (Poole's mom); Vivian Kubrick ("Squirt")

Mid Mar Scribes Launch Attack on Stinky Sinema!

So Good They're Bad

Producer-director William Castle fancied himself a great showman—and for about seven years he was. He rose from the ranks of anonymous B-picture directors in the 1940s and early 1950s to a more rarefied (and profitable) position as a *high-profile* B-picture producer-director in the late 1950s and 1960s. Efficient but unremarkable as a director, he made his reputation with amusing, wildly derivative horror thrillers that were promoted with outlandish gimmicks.

Films from the first half of Castle's career—his period of anonymity—encompassed numerous genres and had little in common except that they were programmers. He had commercial success with three well-done films in the Whistler mystery series, beginning with *The Whistler* in 1944, and directed a modest but effective film noir, *When Strangers Marry*, the same year. By 1953, Castle was firmly ensconced at Columbia and typecast as a director of B-plus Westerns: *Fort Ti*, *Conquest of Cochise* (both 1953); *The Law vs. Billy the Kid* (1954); *The Gun That Won the West* (1955).

By the mid-1950s Castle had directed costume pictures such as *The Saracen Blade* (1954), and moved to straightforward crime thrillers: *New Orleans Uncensored* (1955) and *The Houston Story* (1956).

By 1957, Castle was agitating with Columbia chief Harry Cohn for an opportunity to produce. When Cohn refused, Castle left the security of a studio contract to strike out on his own. His initial foray as an independent producer-director, *Macabre* (1958), was hyped with a $1,000 Lloyds of London insurance policy payable to the beneficiary of any unfortunate who died of fright while a member of the audience. (No one collected.) For big-city engagements of *The Tingler* (1958), selected theater seats were fitted with small electric motors, which gave the occupants a startling vibration during the story's tense moments. Castle dubbed this cheeky innovation "Percepto." (Enterprising kids with screwdrivers stole many of the motors.) During showings of *House on Haunted Hill* (1959), a luminous skeleton was swept over the audience (Castle called this "Emergo"), and in *13 Ghosts* (1960), audience members could view—or block out—the title phantasms with "Illusion-O," polarized cardboard glasses. These shenanigans earned Castle a noticeable place in Hollywood history; even people who don't know his name have a passing acquaintance with his gimmicks, and his spirit was celebrated in Joe Dante's *Matinee* (1993), a sweetly nostalgic look at Cold War movie-going and a Hollywood huckster named Lawrence Woolsey, Jr.

The plots of most of Castle's horror films are predicated on greed. In *House on Haunted Hill* Carol Ohmart covets the fortune of husband Vincent Price; in *The Tingler* theater owner Philip Coolidge kills his wife for insurance money; in *13 Ghosts* clean-cut Martin Milner masquerades as a spook in order to get his hands on a hidden fortune. *Homicidal*—which was created mainly to cash in on the shock effects and bizarre

Adrims (James Westerfield) performs his last wedding ceremony for the imposter Miriam (Jean Arless) and Jim (Richard Rust).

sexuality of Alfred Hitchcock's *Psycho* (1960)—follows this plot pattern.

After checking into a second-rate hotel in Ventura, California, a gorgeous blonde named Miriam Webster (Jean Arless) flirts with the good-looking bellboy, Jim Nesbitt (Richard Rust), asks for ice and then offers him $2,000 if he'll marry her the next day. She's quick to add that the marriage will not be consummated, and that it will be annulled immediately after the ceremony. Nesbitt is intrigued but puzzled: "I understand what you're saying but I don't understand why." Regardless, partial payment in advance is enough to convince Nesbitt to agree to pick up Miriam at midnight on the sixth.

The pair drives in darkness to the isolated home of Alfred Adrims, a justice of the peace. Once again, Nesbitt is confused: "How are you going to get us annulled this time of night?" Miriam gives Nesbitt an abstract gaze and says nothing.

Inside the house, Adrims (James Westerfield), crotchety about being awakened but mollified by Miriam's offer to pay double his usual fee, performs the ceremony as his wife (Hope Summers) acts as witness. The ceremony completed, Adrims pronounces, "Now I get to kiss the bride." At this, Miriam reaches into her purse and pulls out a wicked knife, which she plunges repeatedly, angrily, into Adrims' ample belly. He shrieks with panic and pain, a dark stain of blood spreads across his undershirt and courses over his fingers. The missus screams her head off and Nesbitt stands by in shock, motionless. Adrims staggers back against a doorway curtain and pulls it loose as he falls to the floor, dead. Miriam dashes from the house and flees in Nesbitt's car (the bellboy has conveniently left the keys in the ignition).

This startling sequence is one of the most effective in horror film history. Within the span of just a few minutes, *Homicidal* establishes itself as a horror film dedicated not just to surprise, but also to harsh, visceral shock.

The remainder of the story tales place in the California town of Solvang, a picturesque community with quaint architecture suggestive of the founders' Scandinavian origins. Miriam enters a darkened mansion, washes blood from the knife and informs the house's occupant, Helga (Eugenie Leontovich), a mute old woman confined to a wheelchair, "Adrims died tonight—*screaming*!!" In short order we discover that the real name of the murderess is Emily, and that the genuine Miriam Webster is a pretty, unassuming woman (Patricia Breslin) who lives nearby, and who happily awaits the arrival of her long-absent half-brother Warren. In a few days Warren will turn 21, and he will inherit the mansion occupied by Emily and Helga and a $10 million fortune, all left to him by his father.

And how does Emily fit into this? Well, as she cattily informs Miriam the following day, she met Warren while he was visiting Denmark. They fell in love and were married. Warren's inheritance will be shared with her.

When Warren arrives in town he's delighted to be reunited with Miriam but is alarmed by the increasingly bizarre behavior of Emily, who is moody and confrontational, and who cannot satisfactorily account for her whereabouts during the time Miriam's floral shop and apartment were vandalized. (As we have seen in a sequence that vibrates with anger and violence, the culprit is Emily.)

In the darkened mansion at the climax, Emily murders Helga and readies herself to dispose of Miriam, too, but not before she removes her blonde wig and

Emily's affinity for knives will be the death of Helga (Eugenie Leontovich).

reveals that she and Warren are one and the same! As Emily/Warren raises the knife, he/she is stopped by the timely arrival of the local doctor (Alan Bunce), who subdues the killer.

The film's coda is dominated by a psychiatrist who explains to Miriam and Karl that (take a deep breath and pay attention) Warren was born a girl but raised as a son by his father, who desperately wanted a male heir. Miriam knew nothing of the grotesque deception while growing up with Warren. In time, the psychiatrist says, the strain of being Warren was too much for the "boy" to bear. To compensate, "Warren created Emily, a homicidal maniac who did his killing for him." Later, the psychiatrist explains, "Helga took Warren to Denmark. What happened there, we don't know." Upon returning home, Warren felt the time was right to unveil Emily by introducing her as his bride.

Adrims was killed because he was the county clerk at the time of Warren's birth and prepared a certificate stating that the infant was a girl. Helga was the nurse who delivered the baby, so she too had to die if Warren was to carry out his scheme. If the final murder, that of Miriam, had been successful, Warren would simply have made Emily—the prime suspect—disappear, leaving him to enjoy his inheritance without fear of exposure.

Warren (Jean Arless) has a big surprise for his half-sister, Miriam (Pat Breslin).

But wait: *Homicidal* has one final revelation, which is accomplished at the very end via split-screen trickery. In a stage-like curtain call, Emily and Warren stand side by side and bow to the audience, and a credit line reveals that both roles have been played by a single actress (or is it actor?), Jean Arless.

Homicidal is about greed and violence, and on that level unfolds like a standard thriller. But its special resonance arises from its preoccupation with a disturbing sort of sexuality that we instinctively know is "wrong"—

Emily plans to murder Miriam and then disappear.

Homicidal **equates ambiguous sexuality with physical violence.**

not in a moral sense (other than the fact that Warren/Emily is a killer, the script invites no particular negative judgment of him/her); rather, we recoil because of the ambiguity of Warren's sexuality. Part of our distaste is grounded in pity, for Warren—although born a girl—had been forcibly *transformed* into a boy by his father, and thus is the victim of a terrible crime.

At the same time, though, we're made aware that Warren has become complicit in his own transformation. In the film's final sequence, when the psychiatrist suggests that something peculiar happened during Warren's stay in Denmark, the script is hinting broadly at a sex-change operation—and not the male-to-female variety made famous in the early 1950 by George/Christine Jorgensen, but the considerably more rare female-to-male transformation. Warren has undergone this change of his own free will and because of past abuse that he is powerless to resist. In a strange paradox, the killer is both powerful and powerless. In the final judgment, though, because Warren has consciously chosen to perpetuate his own victimization, he becomes an accomplice to his own corruption.

The final, and most potent, jab to the audience that arises from Emily/Warren's sexuality is the way the film equates ambiguous sexuality with physical violence. The character is male *and* female, both and neither, and thus (the film reasons) homicidally violent. It's this point of view that makes the central character's sexuality not merely puzzling but distasteful and threatening. Unorthodox sexual orientation, *Homicidal* tells us, is dangerous.

Castle originally planned to cast an actor in the dual role. He interviewed dozens of young men, most of them, according to his autobiography, gay and, one may assume, insufficiently masculine to carry off the deception. Dissatisfied with these candidates, Castle searched Hollywood talent agencies and casting offices, looking for an actress. Finally, an agent named Jerry Lauren phoned with news that he had just the woman Castle had been looking for.

The actress was a leggy blonde named Joan Marshall, who had co-starred with Dane Clark in a syndicated 1959 TV series called *Bold Adventure*. Castle described her as "strikingly beautiful" and possessed of "a strange, different quality." She had large eyes that bored into whomever she looked at, a full, sensuous mouth, a strong profile and marvelous bone structure highlighted by a square jaw and high, prominent cheekbones.

Castle was further intrigued by the relatively low pitch of Marshall's voice. After he described the role

Joan Marshall in a creepy promotional photo for *Homicidal*

to her, he phoned Columbia makeup chief Ben Lane and asked him to turn the beautiful Marshall into a man. Castle sent the actress off to makeup. Two hours later, a slender young man entered Castle's office and asked to see the director. The young man was, of course, Joan Marshall; Castle was suitably impressed. He took her to a men's hairstylist in Beverly Hills where her long blonde hair was cut and dyed black. (This part of Castle's recollection seems doubtful, for to cut Marshall's hair before she had been formally cast—and, more importantly, before the shooting of her "Emily" scenes—is madness. A good guess is that the actress shot her female scenes first, and then was given the haircut so that she could do her "Warren" scenes.)

Castle goes on to claim that he had a mask maker he identifies only as "Ernie" devise an appliance for Marshall's nose, and another, more dramatic one, for her mouth, both of which gave her face an angular, masculine look. After taking casts of Marshall's hands, Ernie created hand appliances, as well. If the mysterious Ernie did all this, he did it anonymously, for only Ben Lane receives screen credit for makeup. (Of course, even in these waning days of the studio system, department heads nearly always received credit for work done by others.)

If casts of Marshall's hands were made, they were not featured in the film; in her Warren guise, Marshall spends most of her time with her hands hidden in her trouser pockets, a self-consciously "masculine" pose that is an unfortunate peculiarity of her performance.

At Castle's request, Marshall wore brown contact lenses over her blue eyes during Warren's scenes, and wore dark makeup suggestive of a suntan.

An uncredited actor did post-production dubbing of Marshall's voice in her scenes as Warren, a point Castle neglected to mention in his autobiography. Also unmentioned is the film's clever use of a male double whenever Warren walks away with his back to the camera and when the character is seen in long shot. The double was slender yet clearly male, and his presence reinforces our willingness to accept Warren as a man.

Finally, to add psychological weight to the illusion, Castle changed Joan Marshall's name to the androgynous "Jean Arless."

By now vindicated in his belief in the box-office potential of gimmickry, Castle had little trouble convincing Columbia executives to offer full refunds to *Homicidal* audiences via something called the Fright Break. In the film's original run, the narrative was interrupted about a minute before the climax. An animated clock appears on the screen and Castle's voice issues from the soundtrack: "This is the 'Fright Break!' You hear that sound? The sound of a heartbeat! Is it beating faster than your heart? Or slower? This heart is going to beat for another 65 seconds to allow anyone to leave this theater who is too frightened to see the end of the picture, and get your *full admission refunded*. Ten seconds more and we go into the house [where the climax will take place]. It's now or never! Five! Four! You're a brave audience! Two! One!"

Joan Marshall

In an early screening attended by Columbia executives, nearly everybody in the audience thundered up the aisles to get their money back. One executive was so appalled he punched Castle on the shoulder and called him a jerk. In the lobby, the theater's worried manager stated the obvious when he said, "Mr. Castle, something is wrong."

Joan Marshall, made up as Warren, used the name Jean Arless for her film credit in *Homicidal*.

Castle got more than his money's worth from Marshall's performance.

Castle quickly figured out what had happened: The people demanding refunds had sat through the film twice. They'd enjoyed the climax the first time around, then patiently waited for the Fright Break in the following show. That was a lot of trouble for 50 or 75 cents, but a potential disaster for Castle and Columbia if allowed to transpire across the country.

The solution was to color-key tickets to each showing, so that, for instance, a *red* ticket would not be refunded during the *blue* showing. The Fright Break subsequently worked beautifully, and across the country less than one percent of audiences asked for their money back.

The fear of public humiliation was one reason why. Castle augmented the Fright Break with a roped-off section of lobby called the Coward's Corner, where the "frightened" audience member had to sit before being refunded his money. The Corner was bathed in cowardly yellow light and was attended by a "nurse" with a blood-pressure outfit. A recorded voice intoned, "These cowards are too frightened to see the end of *Homicidal*! Watch them shiver in the Coward's Corner. Coward… coward… coward…"

Homicidal was scripted by Robb White, a glib, witty writer of short stories and non-fiction books who scripted most of the episodes of *Men of Annapolis*, a syndicated television series produced by Castle in 1957. (Castle's other TV production credits are *Meet McGraw*, 1957-58, and *Ghost Story*, 1972.) Castle was taken with White's sharp dialogue and ability to perform under pressure. The pair teamed up on Castle's first spook picture, *Macabre*, and White immediately became Castle's most significant collaborator. *House on Haunted Hill*, *The Tingler*, *13 Ghosts* and *Homicidal* followed.

Homicidal was skillfully shot by Burnett Guffey, who took advantage of the black-and-white film stock by plunging key setups into eerie, disconcerting shadow. He also lit Marshall rather harshly, giving her beauty an aggressive edge.

Castle's direction is briskly efficient, and one senses that he got considerably more than his money's worth from Marshall, whose performance is upsettingly intense. Her turn of gaze, her gestures, her tone of voice and the way she uses her body to invade other people's space suggest a person perpetually on the verge of a violent explosion.

When Emily enters Miriam's floral shop she gazes sentimentally at a tiny groom atop a wedding display, lets it tenderly "kiss" the tiny bride, then suddenly wrenches off the groom's head, her face transformed

Marshall was filmed in harsh light, giving her beauty an aggressive edge.

from tenderness to fury. In another sequence, she enters Karl's drugstore and passes a small boy on his way out, allowing her fingers to trail lightly, fondly, across his hair. Later, she calls a handyman (Wolfe Barzell) to the house to sharpen *the* knife. "I never saw a knife like this before," the fellow pronounces.

"It's a surgical knife," Emily says slowly. "Doctors use it."

"What do *you* use it for?"

Pause. Then, off-handedly: "Various things."

With blade in hand, Emily returns to the house and confronts the helpless Helga: "I never liked your eyes, Helga. They see too much!"

The unexpected arrival of the local physician postpones Helga's fate. Emily slips the knife between the pages of a magazine and makes small talk as the mute Helga struggles frantically to let the doctor know she's in deadly peril. Puzzled but unalarmed, the doctor leaves. A second after Emily locks Helga's wheelchair on the staircase escalator—that will take her to her fateful end on second floor—editor Edwin Bryant cleverly cuts to the human-like screech of the doctor's tires as his car leaves the driveway.

When Miriam enters the house at the climax, she spies Helga in her wheelchair at the top of the staircase. The chair mysteriously begins a descent to the first floor, and when it bumps to a stop, Helga's head (seen by now as a shadow on the wall) rocks momentarily, then drops from her shoulders and onto the floor! Miriam begins to shriek (similar to Vera Miles at the climax of *Psycho*) and cues the entrance of Emily.

All of this is fun, but a viewer with any sort of conscience is bothered by the film's overt similarities to *Psycho*: the fact that "Miriam Webster" sounds very much like "Marion Crane," the name of the Janet Leigh character in *Psycho*; the killer's preoccupation with knives; the working class male lead (Karl is a druggist; in *Psycho*, John Gavin plays the owner of a hardware store); a sequence in which the killer is apparently pursued by a police car, as Janet Leigh is pursued in *Psycho*; a dark, creepy house; numerous shots of people ascending stairs; the presence of a coldly efficient detective (amusingly, this plainclothes officer, played by Gilbert Green, drives a black-and-white squad car); audible but unseen dialogues that turn out to be monologues; a lone woman entering a menacing house at the climax; a final, static sequence that utilizes a psychiatrist to illuminate plot points; and, of course, the cross-dressing and ambiguous sexuality that are vital to the film's plot and tension.

In a 1990 interview with film historian Tom Weaver, Robb White recalled two significant things about the script of *Homicidal*. First, he did not see *Psycho* until he had

with the lantern-jawed producer-director happily laboring over an enormous piece of needlepoint, pausing only when he accidentally sticks his finger with his needle. "The more adventurous among you may remember our previous excursions into the macabre," he says lightly. "Our visits to haunted hills, to tinglers and to ghosts. This time, we have an even stranger tale to unfold. Ooh! Aa, blood! [Castle pauses to suck his injured digit.] The story of a lovable group of people who just happen to be... *homicidal*." Castle turns the embroidery to the audience, displaying the title in needlepoint.

The movie reviewer for *Time* apparently suffered a brain embolism the day he reviewed *Homicidal*, for although he noted that the film was "*Psycho*phantic" and "obviously made in imitation of Hitchcock's thriller," he added that "just as obviously it surpasses its model in structure, suspense and sheer nervous drive. Simply, directly, the camera watches a homicidal maniac (Jean Arless) proceed through a carefully premeditated series of ferocious murders."

The review's praise, which suggested that Castle had topped the Master, undoubtedly tickled the gimmickmeister right down to his toes. Certainly, Hitchcock was never far from his mind: During the *Homicidal* publicity campaign Castle posed with Marshall (who wore a black leotard and pilgrim's hat) for a photo in which he carves a Thanksgiving feast: Hitchcock's head!

completed his draft of the *Homicidal* script. Second, Castle worked with White more closely on *Homicidal* than on any other of their collaborations, augmenting White's ideas with his own. When White finally did get around to seeing Hitchcock's thriller, he realized what Castle was up to. "I was on my way home when I saw that *Psycho* was playing somewhere in Santa Monica," he recalled. "I'd heard about the picture, I went in there and, Jesus Christ, I was afraid I was going to get arrested before I could get out! I was so embarrassed—[Castle] stole everything! And *Homicidal* was already in production by that time. But apparently nobody gave a shit that he had stolen it from Hitchcock."

Homicidal was the final Castle-White collaboration. White had grown tired of what he described as Castle's penuriousness, lying and sleight-of-hand approach to contracts and payments. Further, White never had a particular fondness for the horror genre. He remained in Hollywood, writing stories and books and many episodes of the *Perry Mason* television series. He died in late 1990.

Castle appropriated not just the gist of *Psycho*, but Hitchcock's fondness for inserting himself into his own films. Predictably, where Hitch did it subtly (in *Psycho*, for instance, he is briefly visible on a sidewalk outside Janet Leigh's office), Castle was blatant and self-consciously "funny." *Homicidal* opens

Despite the novelty and ferocious competence of Joan Marshall's performance in *Homicidal*, her career never took off. After returning to her original name, she had a bit part in *Tammy and the Doctor* in 1963 and was cast as Lily Munster in *The Munsters* television pilot a year later. The few minutes of color footage that remain from the pilot reveal that Marshall, wearing a form-fitting black shroud and a waist-length raven wig, played the part in a creepily somnolent way, as if she were emoting from another dimension. She's gorgeous and her interpretation is interesting, but the approach would not have worn well, and is a far cry from the down-to-earth quality Yvonne DeCarlo brought to the role.

Marshall also did "guest-star" work in episodic television in the early 1960s, including the 1962 "Boar Hunt" episode of *Hawaiian Eye*. She seems to have dropped out of show business by the mid-1960s.

During the span of his career, 1943 to 1975, William Castle (who died in 1977) directed and/or produced 56 films. Of those, only the final 17

are the spook pictures for which he is best remembered, and only those he made in collaboration with writers Robb White and, later, Robert Bloch are recalled with fondness. The pictures Castle made after *Homicidal* vary in quality, and continued along the same derivative course: the tense but terribly contrived *Strait-Jacket* (scripted by Bloch, 1964) rode the "old actresses in fright wigs" wave pioneered by Robert Aldrich's *What Ever Happened to Baby Jane?* (1962); *I Saw What You Did* (1965) has structural and character parallels to *The World of Henry Orient* (1964, the protagonists of both films are mischievous teenage girls); *Bug* (1975, directed by Jeannot Szwarc) is a direct descendant of the giant-insect thrillers of the 1950s; and a trio of comic spookers, *Let's Kill Uncle* (1967), *The Busy Body* (1967) and *The Spirit is Willing* (1967) are flaccid interpretations of the dated haunted-house genre that flourished in the '30s and '40s.

By the late 1960s it was obvious that Castle's creative ideas, slim even at their best, had become skeletal. Some of his later pictures, such as *13 Frightened Girls* (1963, featuring 13 neophyte "actresses" playing the imperiled daughters of international diplomats) and *Shanks* (1974, with mime Marcel Marceau as a mad puppet maker) defy categorization altogether. Ironically (or maybe not), Castle's greatest artistic and commercial success was with a thriller he produced but did not direct, Roman Polanski's *Rosemary's Baby* (1968).

Despite his innovative promotional schemes, in every creative sense Castle was a follower rather than a leader. If someone else's idea made money, he would appropriate it without hesitation. That his best films (and *Homicidal* is arguably the best of all) are amusing and very entertaining can be laid to a number of factors: the slick, monochromatic cinematography that was available to Castle at Columbia and Allied Artists; Castle's flair for clever casting; his artless yet efficient directorial style; and, above all, his *chutzpah*. He was apparently shameless and impossible to embarrass—invaluable qualities in Hollywood.

The final shot of *Homicidal* is of a baby doll that topples from a windowsill in a gust of wind, to fall across a riding crop. Because the image is as subtle as a kick to the groin, it perfectly illustrates Castle's overwrought sense of drama and his willingness to hammer his audience on the head in order to get a reaction. Despite the important contribution made to *Homicidal* by Robb White, and despite the enormous one made by Joan Marshall, the film is quintessentially Castle, and thus his alone. For that, he deserves all the credit—and blame—we can muster.

CREDITS: Producer: William Castle; Director: William Castle; Associate Producer: Dona Holloway; Screenplay: Robb White (uncredited contribution: William Castle); Cinematographer: Burnett Guffey; Art Director: Cary Odell; Set Designer: Darrell Silvera; Editor: Edwin Bryant; Music: Hugo Friedhofer; Makeup: Ben Lane; Running Time: 87 minutes; A Columbia Pictures release

CAST: Glenn Corbett (Karl); Patricia Breslin (Miriam Webster); Jean Arless [aka Joan Marshall] (Emily/Warren); Eugenie Leontovich (Helga); Alan Bunce (Dr. Jonas); Richard Rust (Jim Nesbitt); James Westerfield (Mr. Adrims); Gilbert Green (Lt. Miller); Wolfe Barzell (Olie); Hope Summers (Mrs. Adrims); Teri Brooks (Mrs. Forest): Ralph Moody (Desk Clerk); Joe Forte (Bellboy)

Source: *Step Right Up! I'm Gonna Scare the Pants Off America* by William Castle, Putnam, 1976.

Mid Mar Scribes Launch Attack on Stinky Sinema!

So Good They're Bad

Edgar Allan Poe was no stranger to the early days of the movies. In 1909, D.W. Griffith, often considered to be the father of the American cinema, made a one-reel biography called *Edgar Allan Poe,* consisting of six shots. In it, Poe cares for his ailing wife, writes "The Raven," goes to a publisher who refuses the manuscript, then to another who accepts it, and returns with the good news to his wife, only to find out that she has died. Griffith would return to Poe five years later, just prior to directing his landmark film, *The Birth of a Nation* (1915), and make one of the cinema's first forays into the horror genre. Originally called *The Murderer's Conscience* and shot from April 15 through the beginning of June 1914, it was released that August as *The Avenging Conscience; or "Thou Shalt Not Kill."* In it, Griffith would try to capture the nightmare quality of Poe's fiction.

The Avenging Conscience starts with the death of a young mother whose baby is adopted by her one-eyed brother (Spottiswoode Aitken). During the boy's youth, the two have a strong, loving relationship. Years later, the young man (Henry B. Walthall) and his uncle are shown in an office at home, where they work at separate desks. (What the young man is doing at this desk is not clear; he may be working on his uncle's books, but at the end of the film we discover that he is also an author. The nephew is not named, but I shall refer to him as Henry.) The uncle through the years, says a title, has lavished both "time and money" on the lad and glances over at him with a look of possession, crosscut with a cat studying a bird in a cage that hangs directly over the seated Henry.

After these symbolic images, Griffith shows Henry reading "The Tell-Tale Heart," a photograph of Poe, lines from the poem "Annabel Lee" and images of his girlfriend (Blanche Sweet), whom he chooses to call "Annabel." He also receives a letter from her inviting him to a garden party. Griffith subtly suggests that Annabel represents sexual attraction by showing her not in a living room but in her bedroom, with the bed clearly visible behind her. The old man is jealous of his nephew's

love for the girl and wants him to part with her and concentrate solely on work. "I have sacrificed everything for you," says the uncle naggingly, "and you owe me in return a few years of gratitude." The two men quarrel. When Annabel pays a visit, the uncle angrily tells her, "You are after my boy like a common woman."

After this ugly confrontation, Henry meets the girl and the two stroll out in the country by a lake. Although he loves her, he reluctantly decides to follow his uncle's command to sever his relationship. Meanwhile, the embittered uncle goes to a public park filled with lush vegetation where he views a young married couple with their child, a scene reminding him that a family unit, implying love and fruition, is the usual course of humanity. At the same time, Annabel, in her bedroom, sadly puts away Henry's photograph. The uncle, torn between demanding his nephew's full attention and allowing them to have happiness, returns to his house where he prays to God "to guide him right."

Henry, frustrated and angry, sits alone on a park bench. This shot is followed by the title: "THE BIRTH OF THE EVIL THOUGHT; Nature's one long system of murder—the spider, the fly and the ants…"

The young man watches as a spider kills a fly, followed by another shot of hundreds of ants devouring a bug. Reacting to this episode, the critic for the *Dramatic Mirror* would later complain, "Really this has nothing at all to do with the problem confronting the young man, but it lends events a pseudo-scientific aspect and therefore makes them appear more serious." (*Dramatic Mirror*, August 12, 1914.) To the contrary, these shots do pertain to the theme in a suggestive way: They demonstrate the principle of nature in which one creature kills another for its own survival, suggesting that the stronger or more clever will win out and that murder is a principle of life. On this basis, the old and decrepit uncle, by standing in the way of passion and potential procreation, deserves to die.

After the title, "Realization that his uncle on whom he is dependent, stands between him and happiness," Henry returns to his room and falls asleep on the couch while the unhappy Annabel goes to bed and cries. Now, Henry's "fevered brain" devises a plan to kill his uncle. When the old man leaves on a business venture, Henry contrives that no one should see his uncle return in order to avoid any suspicion that he had anything to do with the disappearance.

Henry takes out a gun, aims it at his dozing uncle, but then puts it away. Here, Griffith cuts to a howling dog and ominous clouds, after which the young man retrieves the gun, walks towards the uncle and places

it at the man's head. But he hears people outside and, afraid that they might hear the shot, puts away the gun and picks up a cane, as if to club him, and then changes his mind. The old man awakes and Henry demands money so that he can go away with Annabel. When the uncle refuses, the young man—a title links him to the spider and the uncle to the fly—chokes him to death, while an Italian (George Siegmann), in a tight close-up, peers in through a window. Moments later, the Italian knocks on the door, reveals that he saw the murder and blackmails the boy. This plot complication, however, goes nowhere and would better have been omitted.

The nephew bricks the dead man's body behind the wall of the fireplace, but he cannot bury his conscience. Shortly after, when Annabel, unable to endure her rejection, visits her boyfriend, the figure of the uncle appears to Henry in a double exposure. Particularly effective is a shot of the murdered man, with outstretched hands, emerging from the fireplace. The tormented nephew is also haunted by visions of Christ and of a stone tablet stating "Thou shalt not kill." Such Biblical images, with which Griffith was fascinated, later reappear in *Intolerance* (1916) and *Dream Street* (1921).

When a suspicious detective (Ralph Lewis) comes to Henry's house to question him, he leaves his men outside to watch the house in case there is an escape attempt. During this interrogation, the young man's conscience again plagues him. Griffith, in an impressive montage of close-ups, intercuts Henry's face with the detective's hand incessantly rapping a pencil on the desk, "Like the beating of the dead man's heart," says a title. The director, of course, couldn't record the sound of a heartbeat but he does capture Poe's intent visually. Griffith also shows

Henry B. Walthall stars as the tortured nephew in *The Avenging Conscience*.

brief images of a swinging clock pendulum, closer shots of the hand, the detective's tapping foot, a hooting owl, Henry's hands nervously folding and unfolding and then extreme close-ups of the faces of the questioning detective and guilt-ridden Henry. Griffith also renders Henry's torment by dollying the camera in on him as a garbed skeleton besets him. Finally, the specter of the uncle again enters, and Henry, imagining that he is once more strangling the man, confesses his deed. He grabs the detective's neck for a second and then flees. Pursued by the police, the young man hides in a building and then attempts suicide, after which the heart-broken Annabel jumps off a cliff.

This is in essence the story, although there are some wholly unnecessary plot complications that clutter the narrative. Namely, at the garden fête there is a brief, irrelevant subplot in which a grocer boy (Bobby Harron) woos a maid (Mae Marsh)—proletarian roles that would be fully developed by the same actors later that year in *The Mother and the Law*. More serious and awkward is the plotting towards the end of the film: Henry hires the blackmailing Italian and his henchmen for protection (against what?) and devises, in another building, a secret trapdoor through which he might escape. One policeman who has accompanied the detective finds the trapdoor immediately and nails it shut. When Henry escapes after his confession, he holds off the police with a rifle and, when he cannot open the trapdoor, he hangs himself. (He is cut down before he dies.) Perhaps Griffith wanted to add some action and suspense to his film, but the inclusion of the Italian's henchmen and the detective's aides merely muddies the story.

Edgar Allan Poe

After Henry is prevented from hanging himself and the girl commits suicide, the young man wakes up from the couch where he had fallen asleep and is surprised to see his uncle still alive. He pokes the man's chest to feel whether he is really there and then embraces him. "Oh, such a dream," he says. Meanwhile, Annabel arises from her bed, "Her mind cleared of resentment," and hurries over to see her beloved. Instead of the old man throwing her out, he has been purged of his selfish possessiveness through prayer and therefore welcomes her and agrees to their marriage.

The next scene, prefaced by the title, "The Aftermath," shows the happy couple by the lake. Henry reads from his "successful" book: "In your voice I hear Pan playing in the woods and all the world gives heed." Griffith then shifts to a symbolic scene where, in a nature setting, we see Pan (playing his pipes) causing a mountain lion, a leopard and rabbits to gambol about in innocent joy, accompanied by elves. These allegorical moments, of which Griffith was inordinately fond, have not worn well over the years and were even criticized in their day. *Motography*, although full of praise for the film, thought that it would "benefit" with "less of the allegorical, to which perhaps one hundred feet of the film's finish is given over" (*Motography*, August 1914, p. 270). Griffith was so proud of his film that he did not conclude it with the usual "The End" but for the first and only time with "Finis."

Obviously, Poe inspired most of this film's content. The young man is taken in by his uncle (just as Poe himself was taken in by a guardian), the girl is called Annabel (a reference to "Annabel Lee"), the uncle has one eye (from "The Tell-Tale Heart") and he is entombed in the wall (as in "The Black Cat" and "The Cask of Amontillado").

The Avenging Conscience is an ambitious cinematic undertaking, one that falters by not establishing in early scenes a closer, warmer relationship between the nephew and his uncle and by not making the scenes between Annabel and the young man more romantic. The emotional engagement that Griffith often achieves in his work does not occur here. We do not share the young man's dilemma as much as we should, nor, in fact, do we much care what happens to any of the principals. Here the director

Blanche Sweet

reveals he is less interested in developing character than in conveying cinematically the aspects of a tormented conscience.

Although *The Avenging Conscience* touches on the dark night of the soul that the Germans later would evoke in their post-war films, it does not anticipate their stylized settings or ominous lighting. Shot on sets lit by the sun, Griffith's picture lacks the shadows necessary to create a pervasive sense of evil. If he is not so metaphysical, he is a gifted dramatist who here captures through editing, rather than through pictorial composition or chiaroscuro, the essence of Poe and shows that he could approach the nightmare world, if not quite be comfortable in it. Griffith was drawn more to love and sunshine and happiness than to the darker side of humanity, but this film—one of his few in which the central figure is not a woman—shows that he was capable of more than what some critics have called his Victorian effusions. Particularly subtle was the use of the caged bird and the watchful cat, the kind of symbolism that Erich von Stroheim would later employ more fully in *Greed* (1924).

During production, Griffith heard of a garden fête to be held in Pasadena and asked permission to film it (*Moving Picture World*, July 11, 1914, p. 243). He also used the lushness of the gardens of the public park and the leaves draping down close to the camera to suggest the fertility and beauty of nature and to underscore the sexual attraction between the grocer boy and the maid and also that between Henry and Annabel. Although Griffith in his outdoor work would sometimes frame a long shot with a tree, he almost never placed anything in the foreground through which we saw his players. This film is an exception. Here he also uses settings in a suggestive, even symbolic manner. The scene where the young man takes one final aching look at Annabel after they break up is placed in a formal garden with strictly sheared hedges, suggesting how his life is now constrained; in contrast, Annabel is shown among branches moving in the wind, hinting of her turmoil and desire.

The re-creation of the mood of Poe's stories also prompted the use of double exposures and other special effects. Although Griffith's photographer Billy Bitzer is praised as a great craftsman, his handling of trick work is often faulty when compared to the accomplishments of other cameramen of the time. There are flaws in the double exposures not only in *The Avenging Conscience*, but also at the end of *The Birth of a Nation* (the honeymoon) and portions of the allegorical conclusion of *Intolerance*. (Some of the shots in *The Avenging Conscience*, among them the superimposed clouds, were shot by Bitzer's assistant, Karl Brown, but Bitzer was still responsible for the overall concept.) Aside from such limited technical flaws, *The Avenging Conscience*, because of its immense amount of cutting and crosscutting, is by far the best of Griffith's first four features.

Although *The Avenging Conscience* has its awkward moments, it certainly was the most advanced

Henry B. Walthall

Vincent Price and Peter Lorre in the Poe-inspired *Tales of Terror*

motion picture made to that time and shows Griffith wholly in command of his medium. In its brilliant and unprecedented use of the camera to convey psychological states by means of close-ups and editing, the film is far beyond the theatrical style, then current, of long takes photographed from a distance. The reviewer for *The Los Angeles Herald*, who had felt that *The Escape* (1914) was Griffith's greatest achievement, altered his view after seeing *The Avenging Conscience*, calling it "by all odds the greater of the two, both photographically and histrionically" (Guy Price, *Los Angeles Herald*, no specific date, 1914).

Shortly after *The Avenging Conscience* was completed, a reporter spotted Griffith walking out of the Mutual offices and asked him about his profession. At first, he sympathized with the reporter for having to write about motion pictures, opining "the crime of anyone obliged to look at them daily must have been something awful," declaring that for him it is punishment enough to look at his own productions. Here, Griffith, who had hoped to be a great playwright, seems almost embarrassed about his films and his occupation in general. He complained that up to the present "we haven't had the time or the brains or the money" that the movies deserve (Unidentified clipping in trade press, c. June 1914). He even criticized *The Avenging Conscience* "by off-handedly declaring it 'crude and full of mistakes.'" But perhaps this was false modesty, for he also revealed pride in the film, saying, "People can't realize it, but it took me three months to make *The Avenging Conscience* in order to get into it all of the things that go to the making of life" (Ibid). Even with all the effort expended, he was keenly aware of his current film's limitations. He knew he could do better and was already beginning on *The Birth of a Nation*, his long dreamed of supreme work for which, finally, he hoped at last to have both the time and the money. The horror genre would have to fend for itself without the further aid of D.W. Griffith.

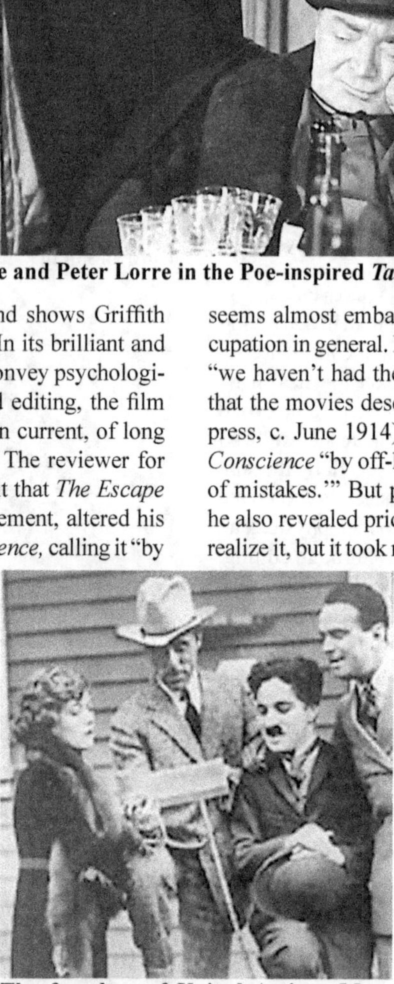

[Note: This is an excerpt from Arthur Lennig's forthcoming book on D.W. Griffith]

The founders of United Artists: Mary Pickford, D.W. Griffith, Charlie Chaplin and Douglas Fairbanks

Robot Monster "is one of my favorite terrible films!"

Midnight Marquee's regular writers have a hard enough time agreeing about what's good in the genre, let alone what's bad. But that doesn't stop them from debating the issue. As usual, this round table discussion was instigated by Mark Clark (**MC**), that inveterate compiler of lists. Bryan Senn (**BS**) and Steven Thornton (**ST**) quickly rose to meet Mark's challenge, with James Janis (**JJ**), Anthony Ambrogio (**AA**) and eventually Jonathan Malcolm Lampley (**JML**) chiming in—while Arthur Lundquist (**AL**) and Cindy Collins Smith (**CS**) offered brief but incisive additional comments. Join them for a tour of "so-good-they're-bad" movies, with a stopover at Mexican horror films and a descent in search of the worst film ever…

MC: I found *Robot Monster* on DVD at the local Media Play for $5.99 and couldn't resist buying it. It's one of my favorite terrible films. This got me wondering… what are your favorite exercises in cinematic incompetence? Here are my Top Five...

1. *Plan 9 from Outer Space* (1959): A predictable choice, perhaps, but a worthy one nevertheless. One of the most hilarious films ever made. Never fails to brighten my mood. Cinema at its most delirious.

2. *The Brain from Planet Arous* (1958): A completely out-of-control John Agar runs roughshod over this daffy picture. Sidesplitting sci-fi.

3. *From Hell It Came* (1957): Featuring Tabonga, the Tree Monster and a cast of dour-looking natives. I shouldn't admit how badly I yearn to see this film released on DVD.

4. *Robot Monster* (1953): Jaw-droppingly inept filmmaking.

5. *Cat Women of the Moon* (1954) and *Missile to the Moon* (1959): I can't decide which is worse, the amazingly awful original or the incomprehensibly incompetent remake! Both provide many laughs.

JJ: Hmmm. If I enjoy a movie, then it is not bad. I do not like most bad movies. That said, while it's

Cat Women of the Moon "is awful."

excruciating in many scenes, there are approximately 50 minutes of *Howard the Duck* (1986) that I enjoy…

MC: I'm usually not a big fan of "so bad they're good" movies, but in these cases I make exceptions.

JJ: You know there are a great many worse films than *Plan 9 from Outer Space*. The damn thing moves and is *never* dull. All movies should be this bad.

I like *The Brain from Planet Arous* and *Robot Monster* (so, by my definition, they can't be bad).

On the other hand, *From Hell It Came* is awful. So are *Cat Women of the Moon* and *Missile to the Moon*. So, for that matter, is *Queen of Outer Space* (1958).

MC: Well, as I was saying, I find most notoriously poor films are "so bad they're *bad*"...dreary, dull wastes of time like *Beast of Yucca Flats* (1961), for instance. *Glen or Glenda* (1953) is another film I find simply boring.

BS: I agree completely. *Beast of Yucca Flats* is simply awful, and I also find *Glen or Glenda* dull.

MC: Then there are films I think are somewhat better than their horrible reputations, like *Attack of the Crab Monsters* (1957), *The Hideous Sun Demon* (1959) and *Scared to Death* (1947), which contain specific elements or ideas I think work rather well, despite these films' numerous other liabilities.

AL: I am rather ashamed to say that I have a lot of respect for *Teenage Caveman* (1958). Ditto *Crab Monsters*. For a movie made with no money, *Sun Demon* strangely lingers in the minds of those who first saw it as pubescents.

AA: If they'd kept *Teenage Caveman*'s original title (*Prehistoric World*) instead of renaming it to pretend it was part of the "teenage monster" craze, it would command more respect. (Heck, doesn't its ending anticipate *Planet of the Apes* [1968]?) Robert Vaughn is fine in the lead, but, even when I was a kid and couldn't estimate anybody's age, I could sure as heck tell that his character was no teenager.

BS: Here are my top five "So-Bad-They're-Good" entries:

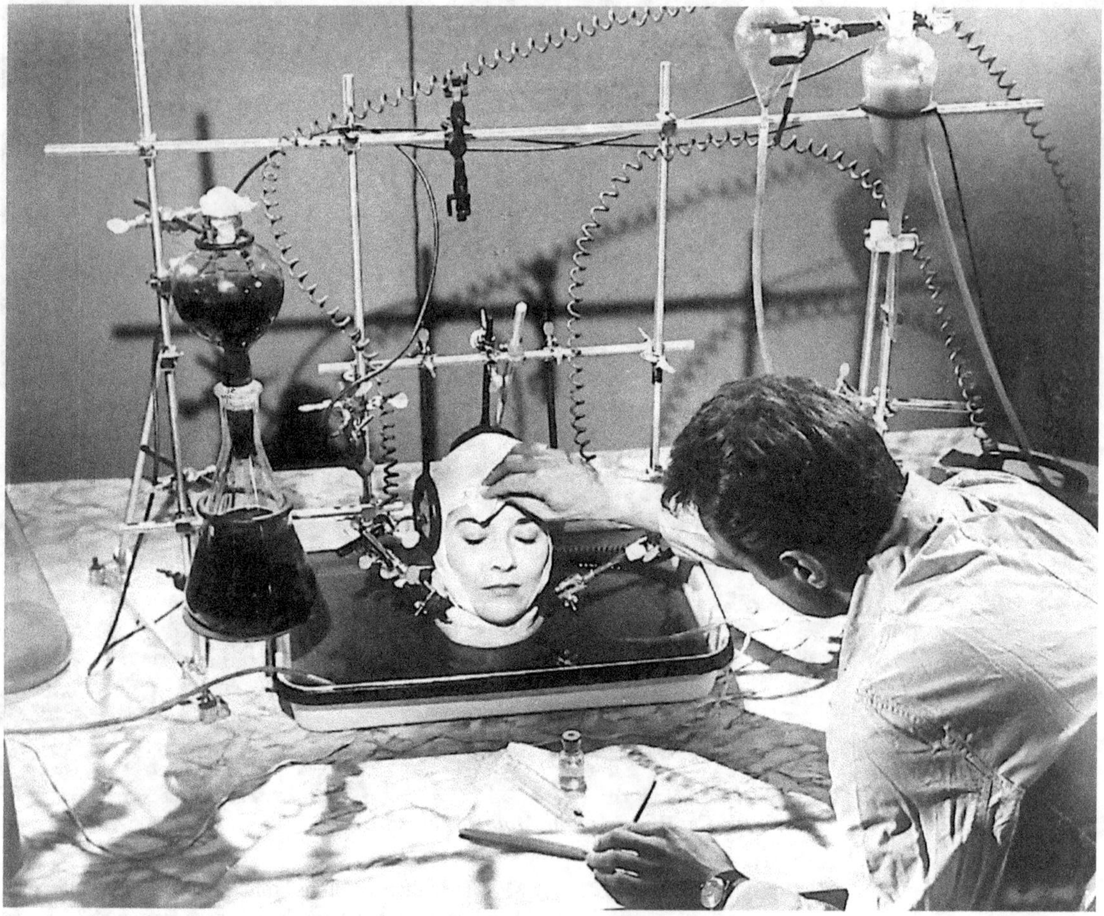

The Brain That Wouldn't Die is "outrageous in every department!"

1. *The Brain That Wouldn't Die* (1963): Outrageous in every department, including plot, gore, *and* over-the-top acting. A bundle of bizarre, sleazy chutzpah that I wrote *16* pages on for Midnight Marquee's *Son of Guilty Pleasures* book. (I even interviewed the director!) That's how much I enjoy this thing.

2. *The Giant Gila Monster* (1959): Love the fun, innocent feel of this, combined with some pretty horrific conceptualizations. (The damned thing derails a *train* for a smorgasbord!) And, sick as I am, I just *looove* those songs!

3, 4, and 5. The Filipino *Blood Island* trilogy (*Brides of Blood* [1968], *Mad Doctor of Blood Island* [1969], and *Beast of Blood* [1971]—not to be confused with the British Hammer Films Blood Island duo, *The Camp on Blood Island* [1958] and *The Secret of Blood Island* [1965]). Wacky, whacked, and strange as hell—full of Polynesian maidens (some *without* their sarongs), John Ashley acting all wooden *and* heroic and the gruesomely bizarre chlorophyll-man and the silly Michelin-man-on-Acid for monsters. There's just something so appealingly outré about these incompetent island-shot horrors.

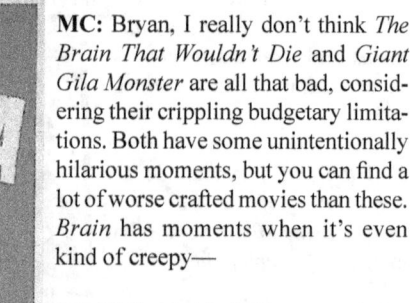

MC: Bryan, I really don't think *The Brain That Wouldn't Die* and *Giant Gila Monster* are all that bad, considering their crippling budgetary limitations. Both have some unintentionally hilarious moments, but you can find a lot of worse crafted movies than these. *Brain* has moments when it's even kind of creepy—

BS: Well, it's kind of you to say so. But they're the Rodney Dangerfields of the genre, as they "don't get no respect."

MC: —but you may be right about the Filipino flicks...

BS: Oh, yeah, baby!

Bride of the Monster is the "closest Ed Wood ever came to making a competent piece of cinema!"

MC: By the way, does anybody else here dig *The Manster* (1962) as much as I do?

BS: Oh yeah, that's a twisted little favorite of mine. Kind of like a low-budget *The Lost Weekend* (1945) combined with a Japanese horror movie!

ST: My turn, my turn! Here are my choices…
1. *Bride of the Monster* (1955). Actually *Bride* is not a half-bad movie, although it would never end up on anyone's "Best of the Decade" list. Between Lugosi's corny yet touching performance and the film's halfway decent attempt at generating atmosphere, this is the closest that Ed Wood ever came to making a competent piece of cinema. I love the atom bomb that explodes in the film's closing moments.
2. *War of the Colossal Beast* (1958). Nostalgia played a big factor in this selection. The sight of Glen Manning's gnarled kisser was one of the iconic horror images of my youth. Throw in a bottle of Faygo red pop and some old issues of *Famous Monsters*, and I'm in heaven.
3. *Earth vs. the Spider* (1958). *Earth vs. the Spider* used to receive continual television airplay when I was young. Rock and roll plus giant spiders. How can you go wrong? Well, actually this movie goes wrong in a lot of ways, but it still left an impression on me back in the day. Anybody wanna go in the back yard and play giant spider?

4. *From Hell It Came*. Mark has already sung the praises (and mostly the curses) of Tabonga. All I can add is that this movie actually *worked* for this non-discriminating movie fan when I was eight years old. It doesn't anymore, of course, but it's still fun to visit when my brain needs a vacation.
5. *The Killer Shrews* (1959). Like *Bride of the Monster*, *The Killer Shrews* is too good a movie to be on a list like this. Admittedly, you don't expect much from such a silly title, but who would have thought

From Hell It Came is fun when your "brain needs a vacation!"

that dogs wearing shag carpet could look so damn creepy. I *dare* ya to sit still when that stray beastie jumps through the door!

BS: You *go*, Shrew-boy! I, too, love this unique and unpretentious little monster movie with just a hint of that winning *Night of the Living Dead* siege ambiance. The double bill of this with *Giant Gila Monster* has to be my all-time favorite 1950s two-fer. (I even have the twin-bill press book cover framed and on my bedroom wall. My eight-year-old son likes 'em too—*Gila Monster* was the first monster movie I ever showed him. He has Mexican lobby cards of the two framed together and up on *his* bedroom wall.)

As for *From Hell It Came*—you know, I really *want* to like this better than I do (I even have a lobby card of Tabonga up on my office wall), but, the last time I viewed it, I found myself checking my watch far too often. It's just...

well... *boring*. Though I enjoy the wacky concept and outré monster, it's just too damn slow when that tree-terror isn't *lumbering* about (heh).

JJ: *From Hell It Came*—*very* wooden.

MC: Well, I've already said that I think it's *oak*ay!

BS: Good one. I've been trying to come up with a pun myself but admit that I'm *stump*ed!

AA: I wanted to make my own Ackermanesque pun, too, but I couldn't be the Forrest for the tree.

JJ: Well at one time or another, anyone's wit can be splintered. But at least Bryan is no longer *board*.

BS: <*Groan!*> Puns like those just *leaf* me *petrified*—*rooted* to the spot! ...I'll have to stop now, since I'm just *bushed*.

In *War of the Colossal Beast*, "the sight of Glen Manning's gnarled kisser was one of the iconic horror images of my youth."

JJ: Keep our President out of this! Perhaps we are barking up the wrong tree. Then again, I sort of *pine* for word play that *boles* me over.

AA: I may be going out on a limb here, but I think these maple-tree puns are just about *tapped out*.

JJ: Who knows? To paraphrase Tolkien, "It *ent* over 'til it's over."

ST: I think I'm gonna take an axe to *all* of you!

MC: Woodman, spare this tree! Remember: I agree with many of your assertions, Steve, especially that *Bride of the Monster* "is the closest that Ed Wood ever came to making a competent piece of cinema."

AA: (That's what I call damning with faint praise!)

MC: I also adore *War of the Colossal Beast*, which is much faster paced and more exciting than the original *Amazing Colossal Man* (1957).

ST: I couldn't agree with you more.

MC: In fact, I like all of your choices, Steve.

ST: Great minds think alike! Or, at least, they enjoy the same bad movies.

You know, it's interesting to note how many of these good-bad movies came from the 1950s. I think this indicates more than just nostalgia; there was something about the market forces of this decade that supported the "bad but good" movie phenomenon. Maybe it was the emergence of the teen market, or the fact that independent producers could compete with the majors, or the presence of an aesthetic that

U.S. title *The Brainiac* "is good crazy fun!"

demanded a certain level of competence even when the necessary resources were not always available—

MC: "The emergence of the teen market" and "the fact that independent producers could compete with the majors"… I think those are the top two reasons, actually, in inverse order.

JJ: "The presence of an aesthetic that demanded a certain level of competence even when the necessary resources were not always available." Steve has nailed it exactly.

ST: We've been down this road before, so I won't dwell on it other than to say that I think a lot of today's filmmakers get by on the premise that if their films *look* good, they've done their job. I expect more in terms of story, performances, etc.

JJ: Yes, we *have* been down this road before. I will only say that I care more about *what* a film is about and *what* is being said than *how* a film looks. This year, I watched many a modern film that looked like a trillion bucks but still fumbled ultimately because it was hollow. Take Blake Edward's *Sunset* (1988), with Bruce Willis as Tom Mix and James Garner as Wyatt Earp, for a recent example. There was *no* excuse for that film to fail, but it did... for reasons other than technical.

ST: Whatever the critical balance was in the 1950s, it seemed to fall apart quickly once the decade passed.

MC: Actually I think the production of ultra-cheap (often bad-but-fun) films was simply exported during the 1960s. Places like Mexico, Italy and Spain became the top producers of wacky-fun, zero-budget pictures. (*The Brainiac* [1961], anyone?)

ST: I'm not quite as enamored of Mexi and Euro cinema as others are, but they do have their moments. And, yes, *The Brainiac* is good, crazy fun.

AA: You know, other than cheap films that know enough not to take themselves too seriously, like *Creature from the Haunted Sea* (1961) or *Invasion of the Saucer Men* (1957), I don't know if I can think of "so-bad-they're-good" genre films.

But (especially since we're on the subject of Mexican films) I can think of plenty that are so bad that they're bad, like *Attack of the Mayan Mummy* (1963), which I once had the misfortune of sitting through. Of course, that's a Jerry Warren paste-up (i.e., botch-up) of a Mexican movie, which may have been better (relatively speaking) than this bastardization.

What would you call a low budget—I don't know how wacky—import of an export, like *Attack*?

BS: I call it absolute excrement. I just re-watched this the other day (one of the less pleasurable aspects of doing a comprehensive book on horror films of the 1960s.) *[Ed. note: Mssrs. Senn and Clark are currently collaborating on a complete survey of 1960s horror.]* I sat through it and wrote about it as a public service: I watched this film so others won't have to! (Sorry I didn't get to *you* in time, Anthony...) You'll have to buy our book to see the complete article (Mark would be put out if I gave it away for free), but suffice it to say that, in 1957, Mexican filmmaker Rafael Portillo shot a series of three related horror movies, all scripted by Guillermo Calderon, within the space of two months: *La Momia Azteca* (*The Aztec Mummy*), *La Maldicion de la Azteca Momia* (*Curse of the Aztec Mummy*) and *La Momia Azteca vs. el Robot Humano* (*The Robot vs. the Aztec Mummy*).

MC: *The Robot vs. the Aztec Mummy* is particularly fun, in a god-awful, psychotronic sort of way.

BS: Enter Jerry Warren in the 1960s, that tireless transformer of horror imports into senseless time-killers. Taking *La Momia Azteca* and adding footage of Warren regulars—such as Chuck (*Teenage Zombies*) Niles,

The Living Head (U.S. title)

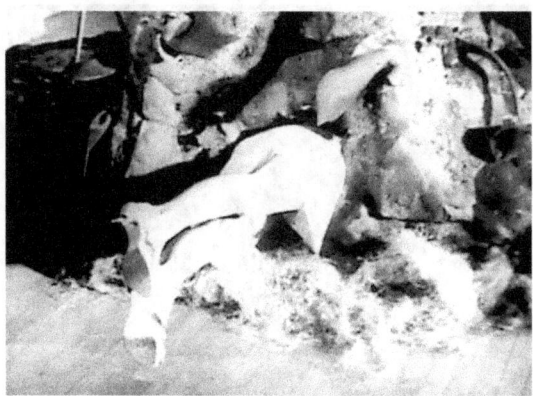

Awww! "A hostile shag rug!" *The Creeping Terror*

George (*Invasion of the Animal People*) Mitchell and Bruno (*Creature of the Walking Dead*) Ve Sota—sitting around talking, drinking coffee and answering the telephone, Warren unleashed *Attack of the Mayan Mummy* on an unsuspecting American public. About half of the 70-minute feature consists of new material shot by Warren, which means that half the picture is made up of lengthy exposition that explains very little, and dull, pointless soliloquies that add nothing.

JJ: Say no more! I think I will probably pass on *Attack of the Mayan Mummy*. Thanks, Senn.

BS: *De nada.* Always willing to take a cinematic bullet for my *compadre*...

MC: But is it worse than *The Living Head* (1959), a Mexican movie imported by that other master of trashy pastiches, K. Gordon Murray? Is *anything* worse than *The Living Head*?

BS: Amazingly... yes. *Attack of the Mayan Mummy* is actually worse than *The Living Head*. —I know, I know, your world has now been rocked to its very foundation...

JJ: I can name any number of films worse than *The Living Head*: *The Creeping Terror* (1964—the one with the hostile shag rug), *The Beast of Yucca Flats*, *Moonraker* (1979), *Superman III* (1983), *Total Recall* (1990), and *Kill Bill: Vol. 1* (2003), for starters...

BS: *The Creeping Terror*? Nope. That one has a folksinger beating on the monster with his guitar! And the most inept Army platoon in history falling over like bowling pins when the creature attacks.

And, bad as *The Beast of Yucca Flats* is, we *do* get to see some kids feed soda pop to a giant pig! And then there's the immortal line: "Flag on the Moon. How did it get there?"

I haven't seen *Moonraker*, *Superman III*, or *Total Recall* in years, but I don't recall that they engendered the painful level of boredom that only *Mayan Mummy* can provide. As for *Kill Bill*, sadly, I haven't seen this one yet.

MC: What can you tell me about *Curse of the Doll People* (1961) and *The Man and the Monster* (1958)? Is either of them worth picking up? Both look interesting.

BS: I can't recommend *Curse of the* Dull *People* in good conscience. It's pretty slow-paced, but it *does* offer some occasional moments of wackiness (a dried-apple-faced zombie monster and midgets in masks and business suits playing the murderous, needle-wielding living

The Man and the Monster

Santo and the Blue Demon vs. Frankenstein's Daughter "slides down the Santo Scale."

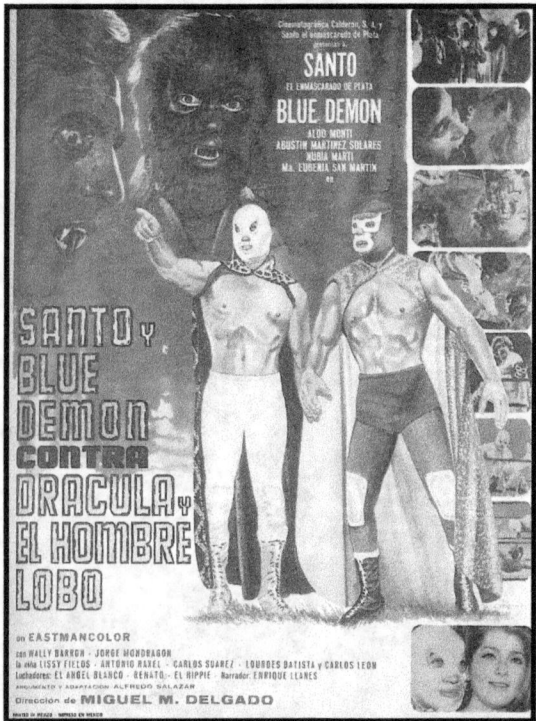

Santo and the Blue Demon vs. Dracula and the Wolf Man "is a lot of fun."

dolls)—you just have to wade through a lot of boring palaver to get to them.

JJ: *The Man and the Monster*? Is that the one about the werewolf piano player? If so, pretty lame... *in my opinion.*

BS: I'd highly recommend *Man and the Monster*. Quite involving and enjoyable, *in my opinion*. It's a Faustian tale of a pianist whose wish is granted, but at an awful price. A great, ironic storyline, a tortured main character/monster and a decent look (with some atmospheric set-pieces). And it's never boring.

MC: Also, there's a four-disc Santo-vs.-the-Monsters boxed set. Runs 30 bucks and includes *Santo and the Blue Demon vs. Dr. Frankenstein* (1974), *Santo in the Vengeance of the Mummy* (1970), *Santo vs. Frankenstein's Daughter* (1971) and *Santo and the Blue Demon vs. Dracula and the Wolf Man* (1972). Are those four of the better Santo monster flicks, or a mixed bag?

BS: I review all four Santos in Jim Clatterbaugh's *Monsters from the Vault*, no. 17 (Fall 2003).

Vengeance of the Mummy is the absolute *worst* Santo I've seen so far. Dull, dull, dull, and with a ludicrous Scooby-Doo ending and a disappointing monster (who uses a bow-and-arrow!). Sheesh.

Santo vs. Frankenstein's Daughter, on the other hand, is chock full of fun Santo wackiness. This one is *never* boring, and one of the best of the bunch.

Santo and the Blue Demon vs. Dracula and the Wolf Man is also a lot of fun—not quite up to the zany level of *Santo vs. Frankenstein's Daughter*, but still worth a watch.

Santo and the Blue Demon vs. Dr. Frankenstein slides further down the Santo Scale, becoming repetitive and disappointing in its lack of monster mayhem. It's basically a rehash of *Santo vs. Frankenstein's Daughter*, but without the fun.

So there you go. Two of the four are definitely worth the admission price (I think they're about 10 bucks each at www.deepdiscountdvd.com if you want to buy them separately), while the other two are really for completists and would appeal only to the hard-core Santo fan (but, for an extra 10 bucks...).

Three other Santos I'd recommend:

Santo in the Treasure of Dracula (1968), which is basically the Dracula tale with Santo thrown into the mix. It's a great combo of that fabulous Mexi-gothic atmosphere and the wackiness that is Santo cinema. This is one of my favorites.

Santo and the Diabolical Hatchet (1964), a truly outré and original storyline (including the Santo origin story!), and a great—and brutal—diabolical villain.

Then, for the sheer boffo factor, I like *Santo and Mantequilla in the Vengeance of the Crying Woman* (1974).

Plan 9 From Outer Space "is my absolute favorite bad movie."

Not necessarily as good as the others I've mentioned, but its outrageous color scheme (Mantequilla—a real-life Mexican boxing champion—wears the most outlandish *pink* pantsuit this side of a *Starsky and Hutch* episode!), homegrown Mexi-horror legend (the Crying Woman), and general charm make it a winner.

JML: If I may add my voice to this discussion, I must say that my absolute favorite bad movie is *Plan 9*, and *Robot Monster* is a distant second. Beyond that, there are very few movies I enjoy watching because they are so bad they're good. I feel this category of film is *very* limited in terms of what fits; I don't put so-called guilty pleasures like *Dracula A.D. 1972* (1972) in here, and many truly wretched flicks like *The Howling II: Your Sister Is a Werewolf* (1985) just aren't entertaining enough to fit. And what do you do with something like the Troma films? *The Toxic Avenger* (1985) tries very hard to be an intentional "so bad it is good" movie, and I just don't think that a film *can* intentionally be so bad it is good. It is an accident of sorts, the unfortunate results of people trying their best with limited resources and failing miserably.

The other day I happened to stumble across what I now rate as the worst film I have ever seen. Flipping through the cable stations, I landed on one of the HBO channels, which was showing *Cannonball Run II* (1984). God, was it awful! Embarrassingly so! People have asked me why in the world I watched it, and I can only explain the horrid fascination in one way: it was just like the "My-God-I-can't-help-but-look" attraction of a roadway accident.

JML: It's impossible to describe how thuddingly unfunny this lame comedy is. The racing sequences are boring, the characterizations are negligible, the plot non-existent. Of course this picture was marketed to good ol' boys and teenagers, but I don't see how either group could stand to watch such an insulting piece of trash—unless, like me, they were held in *Cannonball Run II*'s hideous thrall.

So my previous choice for worst film ever—*The Lonely Lady* (1983)—has been superseded. I never thought it could happen. Wow.

MC: The scary thing is that I've actually seen *Cannonball Run II*. Worst film ever? I don't know if I'd go quite *that* far, but I agree that it's insufferable.

JJ: My worst films remain bad films that *should not* have happened, like *Total Recall*, *Superman III*, *King Kong Lives* (1986), *Batman Returns* (1992), *Kill Bill*, etc., etc.

Up in the sky—it's a bird, it's a plane, it's a bad special effect! It's *The Giant Claw!*

Incompetent slush like *Cannonball Run II* does not bother me as much since these films are such non-films that what is the point? For me, watching *Cannonball Run II* is not nearly as painful as watching stuff like the above-listed films or films reputed to be classics (which aren't), which just make me furious. (*Coming Home* [1978] is supposed to be this great masterpiece, but I think *The Giant Claw* is far better, yet *Claw* is considered *bad*.) But Jonathan is correct. *Cannonball Run II* is unessential viewing.

MC: The whole worst issue is difficult because it begs the question... what's worse, something that's truly irredeemably incompetent beyond description (like, say, the boy-and-his-dead-dog opus *Life Returns* (1935), easily the worst thing Universal ever released) or something that's a crushing disappointment (like, say, *Alien 3* [1992] or *Hannibal* [2001]) or something that's irksome because it's rated highly by certain camps even though it is ultimately a vapid exercise in artistic posing and wrongheaded politics (like, say, *The Piano* [1993])?

AA: (What's the matter? You don't like seeing Harvey Keitel naked?)

MC: All of those four would be on my list of most-hated films. But, then again, the films that are the worst might be the ones I can't work up enough interest in even to despise. Stuff that bored me silly which I then quickly forgot.

JJ: You ever see *Sirens* with Elle McPherson?

Mark: Um, I think I caught part of that on cable once.

AA: (What's the matter? You don't like seeing Elle McPherson naked?) I enjoyed *Sirens*. Nudity and sex—what's not to like? "He leaps from rock to rock with the grace of a mountain goat!" My older daughter delights in quoting that line whenever she can.

CS: Can anything possibly be worse than *Texas Chainsaw Massacre 2* (1986)? That ties with *Spaceballs* (1987) for the worst film I've ever seen. And I'm a Dennis Hopper fan!

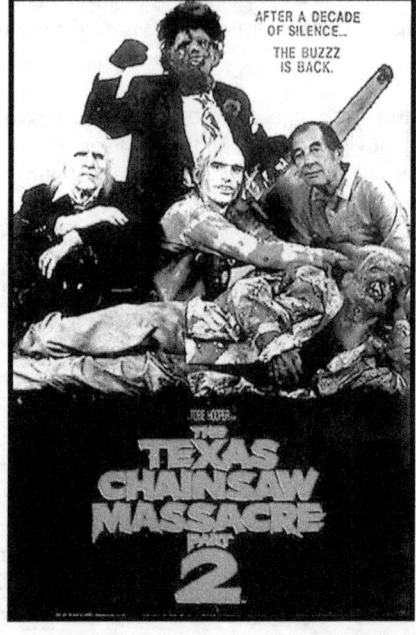

JJ: Incidentally there is *bad* as in incompetent and then there is *bad* as in, though technically well made, still pernicious in other ways.

So are we differentiating?

JML: Well, I said *worst* as opposed to merely *bad*. There are many *bad* movies that are entertaining or interesting in some way. Among my favorite "so-bad-they're-good" movies are *Reefer Madness* (1936), *Showgirls* (1995), *The Brain That Wouldn't Die* and, of course, *Plan 9 from Outer Space*. I think a truly *bad* film is one that has artistic potential and is probably technically proficient but is bogged down by fundamental

incompetence at the script or directorial level. This could be due to some socio-political agenda on the part of the filmmakers, or it could be a simple incomprehension of the audience, the material, or both.

JJ: *Last Samurai* (2003) is certainly well made but still *bad*.

AA: I dunno. A Japanophile friend says that her only problem with *Last Samurai* is that they make the bad Japanese guy a greedy capitalist—the kind of villain we Westerners can relate to—when he was really just in favor of modernization, for better or worse.

JJ: *Howard the Duck* is *bad*, but I still adore every scene with Jeffrey Jones. "*Release the small waterfowl!*"

Gee. This is a more complicated subject than one would have imagined...

JML: It is, isn't it? I say *Cannonball Run II* is now my pick for worst movie ever made—but technically it is better than anything Ed Wood ever did. Anthony brought up *Attack of the Mayan Mummy*; is it fair to compare some low-budget piece of trash with a mega-budget, over-hyped Hollywood extrava-

ganza? To an extent I think you can: many, many films have been made on low or zero budgets that demonstrate talent, imagination, sincerity of purpose and honest effort at entertaining or enlightening audiences.

I guess at the end of the day the question of what makes something a candidate for *worst* movie starts to look a lot like what makes a movie a candidate for *best* movie. And so the only way we can answer these questions is to apply this standard: Did the film work for me? If so, did it really ignite my imagination and enthusiasm for the medium? If so, did it change the way I think about or feel about cinema? If so, then the picture in question is a contender for *best* movie ever made. If, on the other hand, I am appalled or offended by technical incompetence and/or intellectual/artistic fallaciousness, dishonesty, or laziness (the primary intellectual sin, I suspect, of filmmaking) and I am not the least bit entertained, then the film may well be a candidate for *worst* movie ever made. And, if it sucks but I still like it, well, then we have the "so bad its good" syndrome.

Rather a general yardstick, but the best I can do at the moment.

150 YEARS OF WOMEN AND HORROR

SHE HAS ALWAYS LIVED IN THE CASTLE

by James J.J. Janis

The story of women in horror is a simple one simply told; once upon a time, woman in the horror genre, especially film, were inferior and degraded. Pathetic and marginalized, she existed only to be saved from the monster by the virile young male hero who would then carry her off to wedded bliss where she would assume her rightful place in the world... that of unpaid servant and prostitute. Brainwashed to be barefooted, bake bread and be bloated with babies, many of the women in the reading/viewing audience too were only helpless victims of the monstrous horror film which, once unmasked, was revealed to be just another powerful poison of the pernicious oppressive patriarchy.

However when all seemed lost, in the late 1950s and early 1960s, feminism, a virile young political movement, marched into battle against the bumptious bastions of the barbaric blowhards and, after much bra-burning and blistering bursts of bitter bluster, saved helpless womanhood, carrying her off to a happy utopia where her consciousness would be raised and the pornographic horror film would be re-educated into becoming a progressive power for positive persuasion.

It is a happy story with a happy ending. Pleasingly short and uncluttered with any annoying facts or unwanted dissenting voices, it has the advantage of being able both to rally the cadres to action and to keep them in line. No thinking is required nor desired. All that need be known is included and, in point of fact, with little effort, as Helen Reddy demonstrated, it can be made into a rather little nice song. All in all the story is a beautiful thing.

Except.

What if it is not so?

Woman has always been a force in horror. After the genre, as it is now known, was created by Horace Walpole with his classic Gothic novel *The Castle of Otranto* in 1764, there was a singular 14 year period when this was not the case, but, by 1777, as the Gothic movement began to build momentum, nearly all of its earliest primary champions and geniuses were female. There was authoress Clara Reeve who, in *The Old English Baron*, introduced such standards as castles with haunted wings, groans, clanking chains and the rest of "Gothic machinery" that the reader now might view as clichés. This would be the driving force behind the genre for over 100 years and becoming, on film, the Old Dark House subgenre with such descendants as *Horror Island, The Monster Walks* and, not surprisingly, *The Old Dark House*. Reeve was the first to use dreams as a harbinger of terror, thus paving the way for (in the Universal series) Elizabeth Frankenstein's precognitive *visions* and for Fred Krueger. And Reeve introduced to the horror tale sentimental morality, more of which we will encounter later. Women writers such as Sophia Lee, Anne Fuller and Agnes Musgrave soon followed.

This portrait of Clara Reeve, drawn by A. H. Tourrier and etched by Ben Damman, served as the frontispiece to *The Old English Baron* and *The Castle of Otronto* [sic] by Reeve and Walpole (London: J. C. Nimmo and Bain, 1883.

Clara Reeve's novels helped inspire *The Old Dark House* starring Gloria Stuart, Melvyn Douglas and Lillian Bond.

Portrait of Anne Radcliffe

While Steven King has often been used as an adjective to praise a work of fear, be it in print or celluloid, that is through a surfeit of ignorance. If Walpole is horror's Columbus then the Washington is undeniably Ann Radcliffe. Born the same year as the genre itself, Radcliffe's contributions are immense. In her works such as *The Italian* or *The Mysteries of Udolpho*, she created the fairy tale world of breathtaking castles or ruined abbeys set in deep valleys or jagged crags (such as Ludwig Frankenstein's castle in Vasaria and a realtor's show list of Castle Draculas—from the Lugosi original to Hammer's *Scars of Dracula*) and old dark houses set near the pounding surf of an ocean. (As in *Dr. X* or *Abbott and Costello Meet Frankenstein* or *The Pit and the Pendulum*)

Radcliffe created the "hero-villain" who, though evil, is so impressive in mind and almost supernatural abilities that he becomes the focus of the reader's attention and almost sympathy; a character type so much larger than life that it would later demand actors such as a Lugosi (as in *The Devil Bat*), an Atwill (as in *Murders in the Zoo*), a Price (*The Abominable Dr Phibes*) or a Gough (*Horrors of the Black Museum*) to play them.

In spite of all other elements that were before and have arrived since, it could be suggested that these almost elemental figures of darkness *are* the horror genre. It is undeniable that the great monster/villains are what/who the story is ultimately about, drives the plot and whose psychological makeup is the most clearly delineated. The great hero-villain can sometime carry a lesser vehicle simply by his/her own dramatic power and it is this character that enthralls the genre's disciples. Would there be any interest in the Lugosi Monograms if the films lacked Lugosi or if *The Mad Doctor of Market Street* featured Van Heflin in the Lionel Atwill role? Can the reader contemplate *Black Zoo* without Michael Gough or a horror world without a Creeper or a Phantom or a Frankenstein Monster? Even today, in a modern horror world that lacks much in the way of hero-villains, there are the likes of a Jason Voorhees or a Michael Myers to satisfy the need if only on a basic level. With Radcliffe, one can see the progenitors of the great super villains, be it a Dr. Fu Manchu from print or a Dr. Victor Von Doom or a Green Goblin from the comic books—all of which have been or will soon be brought to the screen. What has been called, mistakenly, Byronic should properly be called Radcliffian.

Radcliffe pioneered horror's use of masterly dialogue used as a means of revealing character and of advancing the action. If one loves the riches of an "Even the phone is dead" or an "I stole bodies.... they said" or the exquisite monologues of a "Do you know where you are, Bartolomy?" or the various "Mad" speeches, then it is Radcliffe one must thank.

Radcliffe created the basic dramatic structure of horror with its sudden plot twists at strategic moments, the

Radcliffe created the hero-villain such as Bela Lugosi as Dracula.

The famous unmasking scene from *The Phantom of the Opera* owes a thank you to Radcliffe.

withholding of information or an added mystification. In short, the basic story structure of the horror film's Golden and Silver ages follows this basic pattern: their slow build ups toward the introduction of the menace (usually at the 30-minute mark) and then the twist (the Monster is revealed, attacks or escapes, the scientist conceives of a plan, someone is murdered or the pursuit begins, etc.) followed by the menace discussion/rules scene and then another twist (usually the Monster kidnapping the girl or some type of death trap) followed by a resolution (menace destroyed) followed by the moral/explanation of why things happened as they did.

Radcliffe created the sudden spotlighting of certain individual scenes where the plot pauses to create or increase the suspense by focusing on a certain element. This can be seen in James Whale's habit of halting his films to introduce his main menaces by a series of progressive close-ups or in the grave opening scene in Mario Bava's *Black Sunday*. Dracula's various resurrections—particularly in the Hammers—are Radcliffian spotlights, as is every famous unmasking from *The Phantom of the Opera* to *The Fly* to the shark's first appearance in *Jaws*.

Radcliffe demanded that her nightmares be infused with intelligence and her books are filled with quotes from Shakespeare, Milton and others. Is it even necessary to restate again just how, from the highest MGM to the lowliest PRC, from scripts made up of complex, clever and many times beautiful dialogue to the consistent use of actors and actresses who could actually speak, the classic horror film is miles above its modern subliterate counterparts such as *Jeepers Creepers 2* where characters do not so much as talk as shriek obscenities in a bizarre tonal mantra only the imbecilic could truly find meaningful?

Radcliffe expanded upon Reeve's innovation and also insisted that horror must have sentimentality and morality—in short a respect for human decency. It is amazing and depressing to reflect just how low the body counts are in the great horror films and just how memorable each of those deaths is. Little Maria or Tante Berthe. The villager ordered to shoot the Monster. Gino. Chris the dog. Meanwhile who died again in the fifth Freddy film? Or the fourth *Alien* film? Does anyone truly care beyond the gore crowd and only then if the death was coolly wet?

Seven Footprints to Satan **is Radcliffe as Jim (Creighton Hale) unfortunately soon learns.**

And lastly it was Radcliffe who developed the principle of suggestive obscurity to a fine art. It was Radcliffe who discovered the terror of the unseen or the partially glimpsed or the not shown. The gust of wind. The drop of blood seen by candlelight on a dark staircase. A strain of music coming from someplace in the dark. Radcliffe was "the mistress of hints" who preferred her audience use its imagination. Here is the true origin of Val Lewton and his famous "buses," and many of the Italian horror films of the '60s such as *The Whip and the Body* or *Terror-Creatures From the Grave* were knowingly or otherwise influenced by the Radcliffian style.

Radcliffe's impact was vast. Her book *Udolpho* was called the most interesting novel in the English language. Besides such straight writers such as Byron, Balzac, the Brontes, Keats, Wordsworth, Dumas, Scott and others, it should not surprise that she inspired genre figures such as Mary Shelley, Victor Hugo, Edgar Allen Poe, almost all of the Victorians from Dickens to Stoker and from Conan Doyle to Stevenson right into the 20th Century and beyond. Her work heavily affected the German Gothic horror story from 1798, which, in turn, would influence the German Expressionistic horror films of the silent and sound eras. Radcliffe probably would not have found much amiss with the Production Code of 1934-1967 nor the horror film's Golden Age from Universal to Lewton and Curtiz to the Silver Age's Roger Corman productions, all of which could properly be called The Radcliffian Age. *Seven Footprints to Satan* is Radcliffe. *The Black Castle* is Radcliffe. *House on Haunted Hill* is Radcliffe. Except for the frog, *The Maze* is Radcliffe. She is even responsible, with her tendency towards explaining away the supernatural, for… sigh… Scooby Doo.

No one is perfect.

When, in 1796, Matthew Gregory Lewis wrote his novel *The Monk*, filled with gore, sensuality and a "daylight orgy of horrors," he was purposely defying the Radcliffe school and creating the other side of the genre… the terror story as a collection of "charnel house horrors and lust." Condemned by the Radcliffians (Samuel Coleridge called *The Monk* "a poison for youth and a provocative for the debauchee"), one can see, as what Lewis wrought in his novels and was later preserved in the Penny Dreadfuls, the pulps such as

Weird Tales, Lovecraft, the films of Tod Slaughter, *The Human Monster*, the Hammers, the Cohen/Gough films right up to the Freddy and Jason movies of today, that it was not in 1957 but 1796 that the great Universal vs. Hammer debate truly began.

Let us now step from behind the curtains obscuring these darkling muses working with quill and paper to examine, if we would, one of their creatures moving about upon the printed page before the eyes of the reader. Let us now be introduced to the horror heroine. The horror genre, as early as 1789, has been much maligned by those unsympathetic, ignorant or hostile to the form. Jane Austen's *Northhanger Abbey* is probably the most infamous example where the *Udolpho* novel provides much conversation among the *Northhanger Abbey* characters. And one of the targets of choice—and of convenience—has been the Gothic horror heroine. Even today, within the ranks of terror's acolytes, there are those self-defeating agenda-driven fanatics and their ignorant desperate-to-please flatterers who persist in misrepresenting the Gothic heroine as being some passive dullard who shrieks, faints at a moment's notice and is utterly helpless unless saved by whomever the hero happens to be in that novel. Yet, the literary daughter of Samuel Richardson's *Pamela* and *Clarissa*, all Gothic heroines, is a character who would be perfectly at home and accepted in an Austen or a Bronte novel. There she would cleverly and subtly navigate the rocky shoals of upper class society until she achieved her goals. Instead, in the Gothic, she gets stuck in a haunted castle, pursued by lustful madmen in very bad weather, locked in black catacombs, threatened with insidious torture and gets no critical respect at all.

While attempting to mock, in 1813, one of Gothic's enemies, Eaton Barrett described the heroine thusly, though nevertheless letting some truth shine through: the "heroine is a young lady rather taller than usual, and often an orphan, at all events, possessed of the finest eyes in the world. Though her frame is fragile, that a breath of wind might scatter it like chaff, it is sometimes stouter than a statue of cast iron." She is intelligent beyond reason, can paint, sew, compose, sing and usually play a musical instrument. While, when "reduced to extremities," she might faint "on the spot," she might also exhibit "energies almost superhuman." She may be filled with "tears, sighs, and half sighs" but she can also take "journeys on foot that would founder 50 horses." She can live a month on a handful of food, and trapped in a fetid dungeon for extended periods will emerge finally "glittering like a morning star, as fragrant as a lily, and as fresh as an oyster."

No matter what the outrage, indignity or ungodly terror, the Gothic heroine will endure. Yet this writer would wonder why this is not to be considered strength? This "endurance girl" is usually accused, often simultaneously, of lacking initiative and of being foolish when she elects to explore the dark recesses of

An illustration from *The Monk*

Illustration from *The Mysteries of Udolpho* (Vol. 4, page 217), 1830

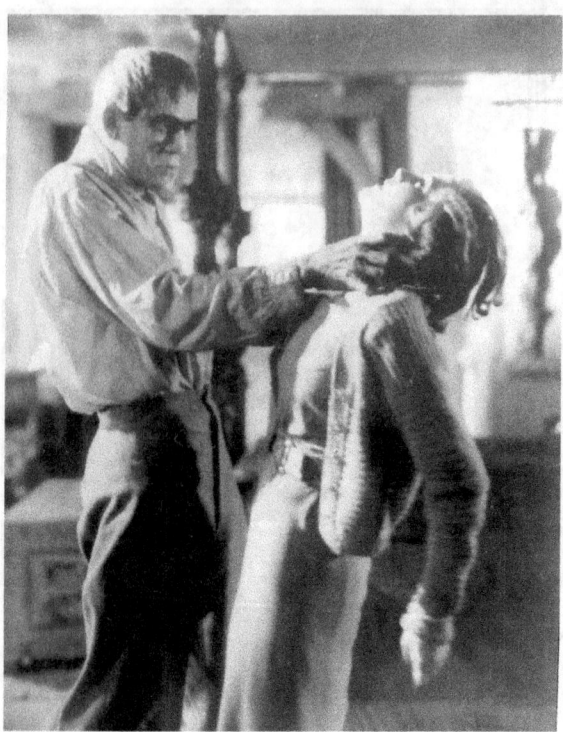

Heroine Betty (Dorothy Hyson) meets up with *The Ghoul* (Boris Karloff).

castles and convents. Yet this writer would suggest that these two libels are self-negating. If the endurance girl behaves intelligently then she lacks initiative. However if she takes the initiative then she lacks intelligence. It's little wonder that she is subject to fits of melancholia and suffers from the vapors.

Author Donald Westlake once derided the Gothic novel as being about "a girl who gets a house." And so it is, but what does *that* mean exactly? The founding fathers of this country recognized that one of the foundations of human freedom and democracy is the right to own property. For with property comes security and with security comes freedom. Every totalitarian movement in the 20th century has identified itself as being the enemy of human freedom by its denial of the right of property. And so, in almost every instance, from Radcliffe to *London after Midnight* to *The Ghoul* to *Sherlock Holmes Faces Death* to *The Strange Door* to *Shadow of the Cat* to, surprisingly, *Hellraiser*, the heroine is set upon by villains preternatural, outré or mysterious who seek to deny her birthrights, her honor, her freedom, her happiness and frequently her life—to make it trendy—to take her away her right of choice. If she gets the house then she has attained freedom. If not then she loses all. The "endurance girl," while perhaps not to the taste of modern audiences, should nonetheless, have her respect and sympathy. The Gothic novel, created around the time of the American Revolution, is about the attaining of liberty from the old medieval feudal order still in power in Europe. What is *Dracula* if not the story of two modern independent women on the verge of choosing how their lives will be, having that choice either threatened or destroyed by a literally medieval aristocratic monster from Europe who, by turning them into vampires, hardly "liberates them" as has moronically been suggested but rather enslaves them, returns them to his castle where they will assume a subservient place in his scheme of things—as vassals—as *his* property. The Gothic terror novel was molded by women; written by women and features women who, through endurance and courage, do get a house and, by doing so, gain choice, independence and freedom. And this is bad?

The Radcliffian model—in terms of form, theme and the endurance girl—would continue into the 19th century. Despite much silliness written about the period regarding women, the Victorian Era would prove to be a remarkably fertile period for women, for horror and for women in horror. In England and America, women began to promote motherhood as being of a sacred importance, declaring that it was a woman's duty to bring about a true Christian civilization whereby men must become more like women and the women more like angels. Using motherhood as the rallying cry, women demanded and received almost complete control of the nursing and teaching occupations. (And it is of note that, besides reporters, the profession of choice of women in classic horror has been a nurse or a medical assistant of some type, be it *Captive Wild Woman, House of Dracula* or *The Gorgon*. And what did Laurie Strode become when she grew up? A teacher.) Women displaced most ministers and became the spiritual guides of their congregations or towns. (Frieda Inescourt's function in *Return of the Vampire* illustrates the concept.) Women effectively removed much paternal influence in the home and in the raising of children (which appears to be what is happening to poor old Kent Smith in *Curse of the Cat People*, what appears to be what happened with Henry Frankenstein regarding his sons Wolf and Ludwig, as well as Lawrence Talbot (implied), Philippe Delambre (from *The Fly*) and certainly—though for the worse—

Hellraiser shows that heroines are still battling supernatural fiends for their birthright.

with the Baron Meinster in *Brides of Dracula*). And anything that threatened their new powers and rights or attempted to marginalize them in any way such as atheism, demon rum or certain types of scientific or intellectual trends would be fought. Perhaps the best genre manifestation of this can be seen in the early cinematic versions of *Dr Jekyll and Mr. Hyde* in which Henry Jekyll is a perfect Victorian femininized man who is undone by his interests in strange unwomanly scientific and theological notions along with the worst case of "demon rum" imaginable.

And women wrote. Henry James would note that, in the 1880s, women dominated the field of fiction—being more prolific and more popular than many male authors. For example, all of the sales of the works by Hawthorne, Melville, Thoreau and Whitman did not equal that of one of the popular female-written domestic novels. Many of these women authors—the most productive ones—were spinsters, independent women—who had a house (very much like the heroine in *The Bat*). Novels appeared featuring feisty independent women who saved men or communities from sin (as in *Strangler of the Swamp*) or mistaken theological notions (usually those dour Puritans—horror's religious villain of choice after Catholics), became writers (*Little Women* being the obvious example here), detectives (the first female detective was introduced in the 1864 novel *The Female Detective*), or were the central characters of such novels as *The Story of a Modern Woman* (1894) or *The Woman Who Did* (1895). In 1890, Mary Bradley Lane even wrote a science fiction novel called *Mizora* that dealt with an all female Utopia that we can probably—ahem—thank for such things as *Queen of Outer Space* and the *Buck Rogers in the 20th Century* episode "Planet of the Amazon Women."

And as already indicated this trickled down into horror. Women had never left horror anyway with writers such as Charlotte Riddell, Mary Braddon and Rhoda Broughton carrying the Gothic flame lit by Radcliffe. Because of their deeply held religious beliefs, it should not surprise to learn that Victorian society on both sides of the Atlantic was fascinated with the supernatural and the occult. (Echoes of this culture can be seen in *Supernatural*). Séances were a must for all who professed an open mind and modern outlook. Many who wrote about the supernatural were, along with being devout Christians, devout believers in the spirit world. So now, instead of evil monks, Italians or Barons, the horror novel frequently concerned a woman who got a house—and a ghost. Films such as *The Ghost and Mrs. Muir, The Uninvited* or

Dr. Jekyll (Fredric March) is undone by his interest in the dark side of life in ***Dr. Jekyll and Mr. Hyde***.

The Canterville Ghost are examples of descendants of these types of stories. And these novels/short stories, written by well-read, open-minded and sometimes well-traveled women, were usually intelligent with excellent characterizations and plotting.

Due to their heavy involvement in things Christian, the moral ground broken by Clara Reeve would become horror's firm foundation. There would be strong moral purposes to the stories, with many of the ghosts being benevolent, rebuking abusive parents or wastrels; *A Christmas Carol*, though written by a male, is probably the most notable survivor of this type, though the films *The Scoundrel, The Ghost Goes West, Beyond Tomorrow, The Passing of the Third Floor Back, The Lady in White* and *The Changeling* can be considered linear descendants. Elizabeth Stuart Phelps wrote novels (*Gates Ajar* for example) about death, heaven and the geography of the afterlife that seem almost certain to have informed such later films as *Between Two Worlds, A Matter of Life and Death, On Borrowed Time* and even Dracula's references to death in *House of Frankenstein* as being a place from which he has "just returned." The sense and issue of morality,

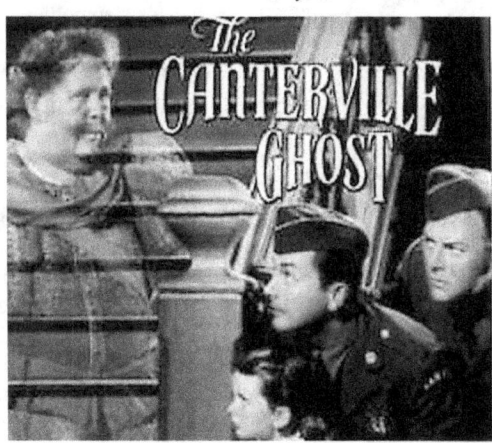

can deny that Quasimodo is a better man than his Master, the Arch Deacon). Even in the genre work of one of the modern nihilist culture's icons, Oscar Wilde, be it his fairy tales such as *The Selfish Giant* or his horror classic *The Picture of Dorian Gray* (both of which have been filmed), there exists an intense morality. Such is the definition of classic horror, separating it from its lesser-mongrelized siblings.

And in most of these books, as should be expected, the endurance girl remained, holding tightly to the mortgage of her house of horrors.

However, soon she would have a rival.

Along with the feisty independent ladies of regular fiction, the bright energetic, jolly girls with a passion for setting the world to right (such as *Rebecca of Sunnybrook Farm* or *Pollyanna*) were the characters of choice in another genre dominated by women authors—what is today called children's literature. At that period though, genre categories were not nearly as rigid, with many writers finding themselves being claimed by adults, children or both, regardless of their own intentions. Writers such as Radcliffian Walter Scott, James Fennimore Cooper and Jonathan Swift suddenly became children's authors, while many "children's authors" such as Robert Louis Stevenson or Louisa May Alcott found themselves being read by adults. And many others were claimed by both camps—frequently genre writers or dabblers such as Wilde, Stevenson, Le Fanu, Sir Arthur Conan Doyle, H.G. Wells, Washington Irving or Jules Verne. Into this genre entanglement, the fairy tales of the Brothers Grimm were or were about to be translated into English. Filled, as they were, with horrific tales of witches, werewolves, curses, murderers, castles and torture, these were short versions of the Gothic novel, intended for children! These charming tales of carnage—though more in the Lewis vein at times—were told to the Grimm Brothers predominantly by educated young women from the middle class or the aristocracy of Germany (and probably, this writer ventures, steeped in Radcliffe) and not surprisingly these stories featured clever perky young girls named Gretel or Red Cap or Maleen who dealt firmly with evil gnomes, witches, wolves or stepmothers—and usually got a house. The Golden Age of children's literature is roughly dated from 1865 to 1910. That period, along with Grimm's Fairy tales, includes fantasy novels featuring dimension-jumping Alice in *Alice's Adventures in Wonderland* and witch killer extraordinaire Dorothy in *The Wizard of Oz*. Likewise, in Francis Hodgson Burnett's *The Secret Garden*, a novel about a young, perky orphan girl who goes to England, finds a tragic mystery, sets the world to right and gets a house (this was later made into a creepy 1949 film featuring a perfectly at home George Zucco and Elsa Lanchester), this perky girl dominated fantasy/children's novels, as her elder sister the endurance girl did horror. However, due to the genre's permeability, the perky girl would very slowly, and as will be seen

Children's literature, such as *The Wizard of Oz*, were short versions of the Gothic novel. The 1939 film version starred Margaret Hamilton.

the explorations of what is right and wrong, not just judged by physical action or appearance but upon what was inside, became the salvation of the genre, preventing it from deteriorating into just a pool of the putrid and the perverse as it frequently threatened to do in the Penny Dreadfuls of the period or across the channel with the Grand Guignol or across the Atlantic with the cynical tales of Ambrose Bierce. The blood of Christ, to paraphrase, was the life of horror, flowing through the greatest works of the period, be it Stevenson's *The Strange Case of Dr Jekyll and Mr. Hyde* or Hugo's *The Hunchback of Notre Dame* (where despite his appearance and actions, who

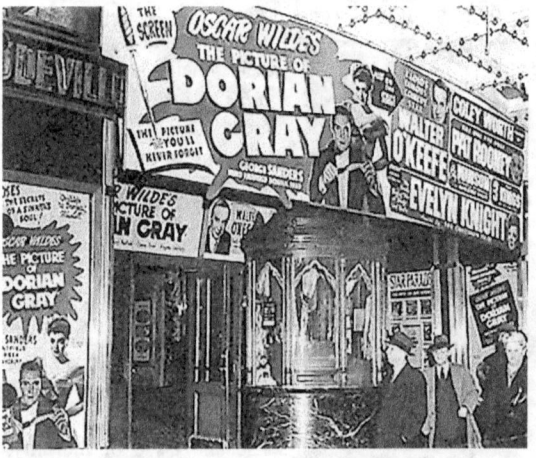

Lionel Atwill and Fay Wray in *The Mystery of the Wax Museum*

with characteristic convolution, begin moving on up into other genres.

The two ladies, however, could not be more unalike. Where the endurance girl was a creature of classical literature, steeped in the poetic and the historic, the perky girl, an amalgam from children's stories, the social and religious novels and the just beginning female detective story genre, tended to personify the modern. The endurance girl would frequently be, whatever her current status, from the upper middle class or the aristocracy. Her boyfriends would be earls, princes, knights or the odd viscount. The perky girl would be from the middle, lower-middle class or the poor. Hers would not be a story of restoration or inheritance but the classic Horatio Alger rags to riches story (or at least an improvement of her situation). Perky girls usually held jobs. Her boyfriends (if she had one) would be lumberjacks, first mates, reporters, pilots or, on occasion, a struggling doctor or architect. The endurance girl would be tall, a tad too thin with classical looks, wear long dresses with long hair (the better to blow gently in the ghost-like wind and reflect the moonlight) and was almost always depressed. The perky girl would be short, sometimes leaning to stoutness, have an oval face with dimples and a pert button nose, wear, perhaps, a gingham dress (but certainly nothing to interfere with her ability to run) or pants—jodhpurs preferred with riding or laced boots. Her hair, when not bobbed, would be short, barely reaching the neck, frequently curled or covered with a cap. The perky girl was always chipper. If she had one (both ladies tend to be orphans, and mother is always, no matter what, dead), the endurance girl's father, a drunkard or an opium addict in debt to the villain, would be just another hardship for her to endure. The perky girl's father would usually be a scientist or an archeologist—who would then be kidnapped by a ghastly heathen cult or the mystery menace—both seeking the secret formula. The perky girl would then set out on a quest to rescue daddy. For a comparison, think Christine from *The Phantom of the Opera* vs. the female characters from *Mystery of the Wax Museum/House of Wax*.

This tendency towards "quests" is a basic characteristic of the perky girl. As per her origins in the religious and social novels of Victorian women, the perky girl is on a mission. Be it to liberate Oz, defend the downtrodden, save orphans or abused dogs and lead

Nell Bowen (Anna Lee) sets her sights on reforming Master George Sims (Boris Karloff) and *Bedlam*.

them all through the glorious gates of heaven, the perky girl *will* set the world to right. As might be expected, this can make the perky girl tend toward self-righteousness, priggishness and a great deal of narcissism (which can make her overlook the obvious—particularly who the mystery villain is). She *can* grate, is preachy and her temper is something to note. (Anna Lee in *Bedlam* or Anne Nagel in *Man Made Monster* are perfect examples.) On the other hand, the perky girl is determined and unrelenting. She never doubts nor questions her God-given purpose. While the endurance girl sort of glides, the perky girl, with head protruding rather like a ferocious fowl, runs to her goals. Like Linda Stirling in *The Tiger Woman* or *Zorro's Black Whip*, she will fly at a villain, fists flailing, unheedful of the odds because she knows her cause is just. She frequently prevails simply because she tends towards fanaticism. The perky girl, be it Nancy Drew or Miss Marple, owns the female detective genre because she *will* fight evil. The endurance girl endures evil, will wear it down and, sometimes, if honor demands, will kill it but she would never be a detective. That would be gauche. The endurance girl, however, can play a lute and read Petronius in the original Latin. Unless her father is an archeologist and taught her Aramaic or Greek at a young age, the perky girl has no patience with such useless intellectual rot but she can shod a horse, fly a biplane and change the sparkplugs on a Model T. She has read the Bible (King James) from cover to cover, though.

Though both are usually young women, the perky girl, when not actually a preteen, always seems much younger and can frequently be a tomboy. Hence she tends towards more action, plot-driven genres. Besides children's literature, initially and still, she would later move into the pulps (Pat Savage, Margo Lane and Nita Van Sloan) and comic books (Lois Lane, Linda Page, Barbara Gordon, The Black Canary and the Golden Age Wonder Woman—the latter the perky girl taken to nightmarish extremes) and, with Edgar Rice Burroughs and Alex Raymond's space operas, would contend with the endurance girl for and later dominate the science fiction genre. The endurance girl would appear in all of these genres with varying degrees of success (she is a regular feature in the Fu Manchu novels for example), but Gothic horror would always be her home.

When film arrived at the dawn of the 20th century, the horror film was born and women were still there. But the situation was different. Film is a business that sprang from commerce and the sciences—not from the arts, the Church, or the hearth. It is a group effort and not a private one like writing nor is it especially subject to morals or respect for family. Women, as a creative force in the weaning of the infant horror film, were excluded, reduced to stealing visitation rights either through adaptations of their stories, novels or plays or through their involvement in external social or religious organizations concerned (especially after the pernicious *The Birth of a Nation*) with reining in the increasingly juvenile delinquent cinema. The result was still that, as creative or moral forces, women, as they had feared they would be during the Victorian Era by these godless hard-drinking scientific intellectual masculine hordes, were left behind momentarily at the movies, while paradoxically their fictional creations, over whom they had once held ultimate sway, were *now* embodied by actresses—a sort of an author twice removed. As Gothic horror reached the screen, the endurance girl was there, making a noble sacrifice to defeat the vampire in *Nosferatu*, surviving Erik in *The Phantom of the Opera* or getting a house in *The Cat and the Canary*. The perky girl, through her dominance of the fantasy/children's novel, would make the leap into the fantasy/children's film (either through film versions of the Oz books, for example or through the persona of Mary Pickford), but her most important move would be in the adventure serials of the late teens and early 1920s. There she would begin to encounter science fiction elements, thus laying her claims in that direction, as well as hooded killers, supernatural entities and other Gothic motifs. By the end of the 1920s, she would be, in (appropriately) German productions, a *Woman in the Moon* and would be setting the world to right with a feisty fire and God on her side in *Metropolis*.

By the time sound arrived, and yet decades before terms

It's hard to imagine Marian Marsh in *Svengali* as anything other than an endurance girl.

such as Scream Queen were conceived, the two ladies became such established types that certain actresses tended to specialize (either through inclination or qualification) in one or the other. It is especially hard to imagine Frances Drake, Gloria Stuart, Marian Marsh, Helen Chandler or Evelyn Ankers being anything other than endurance girls while it is equally difficult to imagine Anne Nagel, Anna Lee, Peggy Moran, Louise Currie, Helen Mack or Jane Randolph being anything else than perky. The occasional example of miscasting, such as Jean Rogers' wildly wrong endurance girl version of perky girl Dale Arden in the first two *Flash Gordon* serials, is only cast in starker relief when the role was finally recast with a wonderfully pugnacious Carol Hughes in the third serial. Meanwhile,

Gwen Conliffe (Evelyn Ankers) in *The Wolf Man* (with Lon Chaney, Jr.) will also endure.

Fay Wray (with Robert Armstrong in *King Kong*) is a major exception, a both perky and enduring horror film heroine.

Faith Domergue (with Rex Reason) in *This Island Earth* personified the perky girl who ruled 1950s sci-fi.

Mae Clarke as Elizabeth Frankenstein kept acting as if she would have preferred helping out the *King of the Rocketmen* or getting roughed up by gangsters rather than all that high emoting that Valerie Hobson would later do so well. Fay Wray is the major exception here, somehow managing to combine many aspects of both types so seamlessly that, to this day, many horror fans still do not know what to make of this strange perky/endurance girl.

As the decades passed and science fiction came to dominate in the 1950s, the perky girl, personified expertly by Faith Domerque and Mara Corday, seemed set to sweep the endurance girl from the scene until Barbara Shelley, Yvonne Romain and Veronica Carlson got a house—of Hammer. Though again, here there is the major and very rare exception of Hazel Court who could play endurance convincingly (*The Man Who Could Cheat Death*) and then be delightfully perky (*Dr. Blood's Coffin*).

The above is no small accomplishment, as the endurance girl is, in spite of some of today's major talents who have attempted to play her, becoming a lost art. In *Theater of Blood*, it is just not possible to believe that the otherwise wonderful Diana Rigg would ever endure anything when she could inflict—thus compromising the film's "surprise" revelation. Kate Nelligan in the 1979 *Dracula* seems to have wandered in from her stage success in *Plenty* delivering a blundering wrong and fatally unattractive performance, and Helena Bonham-Carter in the 1994 *Frankenstein* comes flying in on her broom. Unlike the perky girl, always so very modern, whose very makeup allows her to be both dim and bright, arrogant and admirable, irritating and irresistible and thus is usually easier to portray and moreso to cast (getting a narcissistic self-righteous actress is probably *not* all that difficult in Hollywood), the endurance girl, as per her origins, requires a sensitivity, intelligence and care that, at present, only Jamie Lee Curtis seems to have been able to demonstrate with consistency. The type just may end up like the fictional Miss Haversham and all those historically forgotten female horror writers—all alone in their solitary old dark houses, unremembered, unwanted and unloved.

But this is in the future.

By 1914, it was all there. It just had to be brought to life on celluloid. The heavy lifting had already been done. Women had

Gloria Stuart (with Boris Karloff) in *The Old Dark House*, which was steeped with Radcliffian aesthetic.

staked a claim creatively, establishing much of what the horror genre would be both in print and later on in film. They had given horror the intelligence and intricate infrastructure that put the lie to those who say the genre is without worth. They had made of horror a fountain from which inspiration flowed to other genres of literature and to authors who *stole* the good stuff and then would frequently dismiss the genre with contempt to cover up their thievery. Women had given horror its moral foundations that convey its meaning, beauty and artistry. They had done their work so well that it would take over five decades before horror would actually be deserving of the scorn that has been traditionally heaped upon it. In a perverse way, they had given horror its gore and sex too as Matthew Lewis wrote *The Monk* in reaction to the Radcliffe school of fear. In ways direct or oblique, they had given us *Frankenstein, Dracula, The Hunchback of Notre Dame, The Phantom of the Opera* and so much more up to and including the next film by M. Night Shayamalan—whose work is steeped in Radcliffian aesthetic. They had staked a claim to one of the genre's iconic bedrock figures—the endurance girl—a figure, who, though beset with many difficulties that harry her both in mind and body, with strength and honor will *endure* all to find a reward of security and freedom. Women, though through a labyrinthine route, had created another of the genre's iconic and important figures—the perky girl—who, though fully formed by 1914, had not yet asserted herself. But she would, as always with good cheer and optimism, soon set the world right and become a full member of the world of horror.

And this was done before anyone reading this was born. Woman and horror. She has endured and succeeded beyond what anyone had any reason to expect. And she got a house. In fact, it can be said that—she has always lived in the castle.

DVD REVIEWS
by Gary J. Svehla

RATINGS: 4: Excellent; 3: Good; 2: Fair; 1: Poor

It Came from Beneath the Sea
[Columbia Pictures DVD]
Movie: 2.0; Disc: 3.0

Monster movies released during the 1950s might still have a childish charm, but far too many of them suffer from the very components that doom *It Came from Beneath the Sea*, one of the first movies to feature special visual effects created by Ray Harryhausen, the only single kudos-earning aspect of the movie. Show me Ed Wood's *Bride of the Monster*, show me the visually delightful *Invaders from Mars* or show me the over-the-top *The Brain from Planet Arous*, all three are low-budget B delights. But why is *It Came from Beneath the Sea* such a drag?

First of all, science fiction movies made during this post-WWII era involve plots heavy on flaunting military hardware, in this case a naval submarine, and when early in the film the giant octopus attacks the submerged vessel, the audience is stingily given 60 seconds worth of suspense and five minutes' worth of deadly dull science-babble.

Of course we have the standard at-sea attack where unwary fisherman meet a few seconds of stunning monster footage with minutes of terrified close-ups and a ship rocking to and fro upon a choppy, studio-bound miniature ocean.

And, oh yes, the characters are always stiff with the distinguished but not quite youthful Kenneth Tobey romancing the sexy young scientist Faith Domergue. Far too much plot time is wasted showing time-filling restaurant sequences where the bull-headed military professional busts heads with the equally passionate and narrowly focused scientist. Somehow the animal desires of the humans overcome their intellectual differences.

Perhaps the best sequence, other than the climatic giant monster attack on San Francisco harbor, is the moody beach sequence where the bathing-suited hero and heroine wait for the first sign of the fiend. The sequence is filmed and edited for maximum suspense and this anticipated fright becomes a shining moment in an otherwise dull enterprise. Of course the payoff is the fabulous monster vs. the unsuspecting city final sequence, which features most of the movie's budget in these marvelous special effects that last all of 15 minutes. However, for even a short 78-minute B feature, far too much time is wasted simply sitting around and waiting for the octopus to begin its monstrous human feeding frenzy. Simply put, in many such 1950s monster programmers, the final payoff seldom warrants all the dead characterizations, talky dialogue, intrusive and unbelievable romantic sequences and the focusing on dull military hardware. Ray Harryhausen created the special visual effects for some marvelous movies, but unfortunately, this is not one of them.

Extras include a pristine, widescreen, deep-contrast print, a featurette (*The Ray Harryhausen Chronicles*) and theatrical trailers. *It Came from Beneath the Sea* is not the worst sci-fi monster romp ever filmed, but it seldom rises above the mediocre.

The Beast from 20,000 Fathoms
[Warner Home Video]
Movie: 2.5; Disc: 3.0

Unfortunately, the black-and-white Harryhausen movies do not hold up well by today's standards. They remain marvelous Saturday afternoon children's matinee fodder, and for those of us who grew up watching those grand monster epics of the 1950s, *The Beast from 20,000 Fathoms* still manages to entertain. But the film is memorable only for its episodic monster set pieces and grinds to a listless stop during all the other sequences. Count the five memorable scenes—the revived monster in the snow-covered Arctic is witnessed by one man with a broken leg, who lies helpless as his buddy attempts to save him—then an avalanche occurs; the monster attacks an unsuspecting fishing vessel, cuddling the ship in its claws and sinking it within seconds; the exploratory diving bell inhabited by the good-natured Cecil Kellaway descends beneath the black water and is savagely attacked by the privacy-seeking prehistoric beast; the all-too brief lighthouse sequence where the monster, attracted by the bright light, comes ashore and tears the lighthouse down; and finally, the prehistoric monster attacks New York City and climaxes with the Coney Island roller coaster death sequence. Admittedly, these special effects scenes are iconic and masterful and here Harryhausen comes closest to approximately what his mentor Willis O'Brien did with the *King Kong* series. Novice Harryhausen had not learned how to imbue his monster with personality as of yet, but the sequence where the monster chews up a policeman is one of Harryhausen's most memorable.

The sequences with hardly-noticeable Kenneth Tobey and Paul Christian are pedestrian and heroine Paula Raymond's character and performance is generic and mostly forgettable. Those agonizingly talky, long sequences in the lab are sleep inducing. Perhaps this movie was a product of its time, made on a budget, at a time when children not of the MTV generation were willing to endure long, tedious sequences punctuated with brief moments of monster glory. Today, to the adult eye, *Beast from 20,000 Fathoms* is a yawn whose only redeeming features are some quaint (yet masterful) special effects sequences of a magnificent monster from before time began. Perhaps it should be noted that *Godzilla* was made and released in Japan one year later and that many sequences of the prehistoric monster amuck in the big city may have indeed inspired the Toho classic.

The DVD extras are many, including two documentaries (*The Rhedosaurus and the Roller Coaster* and *Harryhausen and Bradbury: An Unfathomable Friendship*), Harryhausen trailers and production notes. The gorgeous 35mm print used has deep contrast and sharp focus, making the film experience satisfying. But while Harryhausen does fantastic special effects, his framing movies never quite live up to expectations.

The Black Scorpion
[Warner Home Video]
Movie: 2.0; Disc: 3.5

The major flaw of 1950s giant monster movies has always been too much talk, and not enough monster action. *The Black Scorpion*, Warner Bros.' 1957 release, features a Mexican cast of virtual unknowns plus sci-fi headliners Richard Denning and Mara Corday. The special effects, co-designed by the master Willis O'Brien and Pete Peterson, are front and center with many sequences showcasing the giant stingers. However, every time I see this movie, I fall asleep—three times over a 30-year period in the cellar of George Stover who projects his personal 16mm print once every 10 years, and I fell asleep when I recently watched the DVD. And now I think I know why.

The movie is at its absolute best during the initial 15 minutes when American scientist Richard Denning and his Mexican partner are investigating the ruins of rural villages deserted/destroyed by a volcanic eruption. While we see no mutant scorpions, we do hear their high-pitched whirl. What director Edward Ludwig does create is suspense and anticipatory dread. The humans find a deserted police car half crushed, and the dead policeman is found, eerily standing erect with a look of horror on his face. He holds his pistol in his hand, all the cartridges discharged. With creepy photography, quick shock editing and set design well lit for maximum mood, *The Black Scorpion* offers a fantastic beginning.

Once the typical bland romance subplot develops with Richard Denning coming to the assistance of rancher Mara Corday, who is trying to protect her cattle, we finally see the insect rascals attack through the ranch fences and walls. The stop-motion models are rather horrifying and the special effects, supposedly created in O'Brien's garage /special effects studio, are quite effective but in a very low-budget sense. What is not so effective are numerous close-ups of the scorpions, cheap papier-mâché models with bulging eyeballs and rapidly moving pinchers that look fairly ridiculous. And what cheapens the marvelous special effects even further is the absolutely poor lighting used to shoot the giant insect monsters. Supposedly, Willis O'Brien wished to end *King Kong*, not on the Empire State building, but in a sports stadium, and during the climax of *The Black Scorpion* O'Brien finally gets his wish. However, the final surviving scorpion fighting tanks and military weapons is so dark and undefined that the dramatic intensity of the sequence is compromised. Often the scorpions are shown in complete silhouette and we wonder whether models were even necessary if the lighting and photography failed to showcase the stop motion effects. Thus, the plot and subplots are dull, and even the monster effects sequences are dull because of how they were photographed, so *The Black Scorpion* ultimately becomes one big yawn by wasting such creative special effects executed by Willis O'Brien.

Fortunately the print is pristine, and the DVD extra features are quite extraordinary. We have trailers of this film with other Ray Harryhausen movies. We have a documentary featuring Ray Harryhausen. We even have the Ray Harryhausen/ Willis O'Brien special effects sequence from *The Animal World*, featuring a beautiful color print. But most exciting of all, we have test footage found in the trunk of Pete Peterson, after his death, containing 16mm test footage created by O'Brien and him for two potential projects: "The Las Vegas Monster" (striking monster footage) and the "Bettlemen" full color footage. These test footage sequences are alone worth the cost of the package.

While *The Black Scorpion* is overall bland and dull, the special effects footage created by Willis O'Brien (especially the long sequence at the bottom of the cave where Denning finds a nest of the monsters) is quite effective if sometimes undermined by poor lighting and photography.

**Doctor of Doom
Wrestling Women vs.
The Aztec Mummy**
[Something Weird Video/
Image Entertainment]
Movie (*Doctor* 2.0;
Wrestling Women: 2.0);
Disc: 3.5

Imagine both my elevation and disappointment when I heard that Something Weird Video was releasing on DVD the entire line of Mexican produced horror titles redubbed and released to TV through K. Gordon Murray during the 1960s. And then, even before the first release (and perhaps final release), Image announced that problems surfaced over who holds the rights to the K. Gordon Murray Mexican marvels and the series' release has been put on indefinite hold. Drat!

Since these Mexican horror/cult epics were released directly to American TV, the prints used here are good 16mm prints, not pristine 35mm, so the image is rather soft, the contrast reflects more grays than blacks and the soundtrack is far from crystal-clear. However, such B productions do not suffer too much from such a presentation, as our memories of them from small and grainy television screens were not any better, and perhaps considering reception problems, much worse.

Doctor of Doom is less well known than *Wrestling Women* but is perhaps the better film of the two, if we are forced to distinguish between B programmers that are very similar in plot and execution. *Doctor of Doom* involves our old reliable mad scientist who is working out the bugs on female brain transplants. The dubbing is ridiculously funny, featuring those dramatic deadpan voices sputtering forth the most inane dialogue. At first the doctor feels his female experiments die because he needs to operate on more intelligent women, so he kidnaps one, transfers her brain and she too dies. Thus, he figures it out—he needs to use physically stronger women as his experiments, so he eyes up the female wrestling champion, Gloria Venus, as his intended victim. However, Gloria Venus and wrestling partner Golden Rubi generally kick the butt of the Doctor of Doom and his henchmen, even when the good doctor employs his secret weapon Gomar, the blatantly silly offspring of the first successful male/gorilla brain transplant, a human of enormous physical strength. But whenever the villains attack, the wrestling tag-team spins into action making *Doctor of Doom* look like a South of the Border Republic serial.

Since the identity of the villainous doctor, who wears a mask, is unknown, the plot soon creates a slew of red-herrings, and even after the good Doctor of Doom is scarred by an acid bath, his identify is still not immediately revealed, [Spoiler Alert] but of course a kindly, benevolent 40-something-year-old man who moves and acts like he is 70 turns out to be more than simply a red-herring. *Doctor of Doom* becomes exciting kiddie-matinee Saturday night horror host fodder, and the equally enjoyable *Wrestling Women vs. The Aztec Mummy* offers more of the same, a double-blast of South of the Border Gothic fun.

The extras, as is true with most Something Weird Video DVD releases, are extensive, offering 60-second TV spots for the entire intended Mexican menagerie, trailers for many Mexican horror chillers and episode three of the monster, musical children-oriented TV show, *Ghoul A-Go-Go*. With any luck Something Weird Video and Image will work out the details to again release the entire line of K. Gordon Murray Mexican horror classics, but for now, we have to be satisfied with this Rene Cardona-directed double-bill treat.

**The Thing
(From Another World)**
[Warner Home Video]
Movie: 3.5; Disc: 3.0

It doesn't matter if Christian Nyby (the credited director) or producer Howard Hawks directed *The Thing*, for it is a landmark entry in both the science fiction and horror film genres, a movie that posed the original question: But it is science fiction or horror? The answer is that it is both, but it is more essential to the horror film genre that embraces it as the first modern example of science fiction horror. Simply stated, we have the sci-fied image of both Dracula (the veggie creature lives on human blood) and Frankenstein (its lumbering, silhouetted image resembling Karloff's classic creation) coming to Earth via flying saucer, crashing into Arctic ice.

Surprising, while *The Thing* has always been noted for its marvelous use of overlapping dialogue (another essential trademark for director Howard Hawks), it remains a tremendously talky movie, a movie that is almost too talky for its own good. Those military and scientific supporting characters are always interesting, but the sequences of action are scant and those sequences of men sitting around and shooting the breeze are considerable. It is truly the repartee between the essential cast of characters—Kenneth Tobey's wizened military captain, Dewey Martin's youthful second banana always with that gleam in his eye, Robert Cornthwaite's obsessed scientist who only wants to communicate with the alien and Douglas Spencer's long and lanky journalist Scotty, prone to fainting and unable to even snap a photo of the alien predator—that makes the movie snap, crackle and pop. For a film with so much dialogue, surprisingly, the characterizations are always interesting (even the cold-as-ice Margaret Sheridan performance as Nikki) and the suspense intense (although the film's major action sequences only include the Thing melting from the ice and fighting the dogs outside in long shot, the Thing on fire, the Thing's sudden appearance at the greenhouse door and the finale where the military finally fries the Thing). James Arness looks menacing as the outer space carrot, but to be honest, any stuntman could have done the job as well. But it is a shame that the distinguished Howard Hawks, whose classic film resume includes screwball comedies, film noir and Westerns, did not work in horror more often, as the production establishes all the requisite components necessary: isolated and claustrophobic setting, sporadic quick glimpses of the fiend, a character-driven plot, the creation of an underlying tension that permeates the production suggesting greenhouse reproduction of a planetful of veggie predators that will overrun the Earth in a short period of time (feeding on our life's blood). While *The Thing* is wonderful at its 87-minute original edit, it might be even better at its re-release edit of 81 minutes that makes the film move faster and seem even tighter.

The fine-grain print used on this Warner Home DVD release of *The Thing* is marvelous, with intense blacks. Some hardly noticeable replacement footage (restoring the film to its 87-minute original running time) seems one generation away from the rest of the print, but the film hasn't looked this good since the 1950s. Besides a well-worn trailer, no extras appear.

Metropolis
[Kino on Video]
Movie: 4.0; Disc: 4.0

I am thoroughly convinced that the medium of DVD home video drives film restoration (cable channels such as TCM also encourage such money to be spent), as so many well-worn classics of the past are being digitally restored and released to home video, looking as though 60 years of wear and age have been removed. Fritz Lang's early classic of science fiction cinema, *Metropolis*, has been released by Kino on Video restored to 124 minutes (using new inter-titles to segue between still missing sequences—sequences, I am sure, never to be found), the longest release print of the movie ever to surface in modern times. And the restored print looks absolutely gorgeous, better even than the tinted and rock-scored Giorgio Moroder 80-minute version released two decades ago. For me, seeing this two-hour plus version of *Metropolis* is akin to seeing it for the first time, and now I better understand its classic status.

The film's thesis—there can be no understanding between the hands and the brain unless the heart acts as mediator—is perhaps too often popping up as an inter-title on the screen, but its handling within the context of the film is subtle and emotionally gripping. Today, in our modern world of technology gone evil, with the great clashes between the corporate mentality and the worker drones who toil their whole lives only to lose their jobs (downsizing or elimination of the position) on a whim, makes the imagery of *Metropolis* that much more poignant. It is amazing for a film released in 1927 to encompass similar themes of the death of individualism in 2004. Just looking at the workers who march in rhythm to and from the factory, looking more zombified than any image in any Val Lewton or George Romero movie, shift workers who assume positions at the hands of a giant clock whose arms they must constantly manipulate, strikes a chord of truth within all of us today.

The chasm between the rich corporate owners who live in an above-ground futuristic dream city (looking surprisingly like the modern New York City) and the working class who dwell in depressing underground cities still rings true again reflecting American society with its ever widening divide between the world of the haves and the world of the have-nots. The visual richness of this classic futuristic worldview is almost mesmerizing and the well-crafted cinematography, by Karl Freund, lingers in the mind long after the movie has ended.

But the performances are equally impressive, especially Brigitte Helm's dual performance as Maria the liberator and the insidious and subversive robot turned human. The initial images, almost religious in a brightly lit Joan of Arc sort of way, introduce perhaps the most innocent visage of Helm's underground leader who seeks to organize the workers for a better, richer way of life. In contrast, once the female robot has been made human in the image of Brigitte Helm, she now features a snarling, curling lip, blackened eyes and an aura of manipulative evil that never could radiate from the formerly religious martyr. Without speaking a word of dialogue, the dual-character contrast within Brigitte Helm is cinematic acting of the highest order.

Fritz Lang created many classic movies, but perhaps this gem of the silent movie era, *Metropolis*, may well be his shining achievement. And this Kino on Video restoration release makes the diamond sparkle like it never has before. Besides featuring a stunning print with restoration of its original score, extras include two long documentaries on both the making of the film and its modern restoration, photo galleries, cast and crew bios, 5.1 Dolby Digital surround track, audio commentary, etc. Simply stated, *Metropolis*' release may well be the DVD release of the year and perhaps the decade. This is essential viewing for any fan of classic fantasy and science fiction.

**Countess Dracula
The Vampire Lovers**
[MGM Midnite Movies DVD]
Movie:
Countess 2.5
Vampire Lovers 3.0
Disc: 3.5

For a short time during the 1970s, Ingrid Pitt became the female horror movie icon for Hammer films and other production companies, her presence and performances not properly assessed at the time. We generally think of Anchor Bay when it comes to pristine widescreen release prints of Hammer films, but these Hammer/American International co-productions belong to MGM, and their widescreen release on DVD, double-billed, is cause for celebration (at only a $15 list price that generally means the disc sells for $9.95). The fact that the letterboxed release prints are uncut and pristine (unfortunately, only *The Vampire Lovers* has been anamorphically enhanced for 16:9 monitors), equaling anything Anchor Bay has released, is an additional plus.

Ingrid Pitt, portraying the evil Countess who bathes in the blood of virgins, acting under heavy layers of age makeup, only to emerge as her sensual self after taking bloodbaths, creates a nuanced and rich performance. As the Countess, mostly mute and hidden partially beneath a veil that covers her head, Ingrid Pitt slightly hunches over and moves stiffly to demonstrate her frail condition. But after emerging in the guise of her "daughter," after the actual daughter is murdered, Ingrid Pitt glows with a radiant sensuality that loves the camera. Never has Pitt looked more alluring or beautiful.

Countess Dracula, with its stark sequence of the nude Ingrid Pitt emerging from her tub, dripping blood as she attempts to hide her nudity, is a sequence for the ages. Unfortunately, this talky costume drama likes to shock us with the discovery of sexy nude virgin bodies in the closet, and the set-up for murder is nicely atmospheric, but simply stated, the movie plays out at a much too slow pace and the costume drama becomes too classy for its own good. Nigel Green, shortly before his suicide, submits another aristocratic performance that commands attention, but poor unfortunate hero (although he is tainted by enjoying the pleasures of the village prostitute after seemingly committing to the Countess' "daughter") Sandor Eles dies unfairly in the final minute of the movie before the irate villagers punish their Countess Dracula once and for all. However, for Ingrid Pitt, her performance is mesmerizing and quite solid with a remarkable contrast between her non-sexual Countess and blatantly erotic transformation into nude romper. At FANEX 8 Pitt told a hilarious story about Eles' difficulty filming a love scene with her during this film.

However, *The Vampire Lovers* is Pitt's classic horror portrayal and a film that grows richer with age. Touting direction by Roy Ward Baker and featuring a generally uninspired supporting performance by Peter Cushing (just compare his role here as the General to his Baron Frankenstein performances or Van Helsing in his Terence Fisher-directed Dracula movies), *The Vampire Lovers* is not Terence Fisher's style of vampire fandango. Featuring lush period detail and costuming, *The Vampire Lovers* brings erotica to Hammer's vampire mythology, and does it quite tastefully. Ingrid Pitt, through the course of the movie, plays the same vampiric character operating under two different identities, both involving her so-called aunt leaving her at the home of an unsuspecting aristocrat, to befriend a virginal daughter, who will ultimately become her next victim (even though Ingrid Pitt claims in printed interviews that vampires are not sexually motivated, all her primary victims are female and are slowly seduced, more so than attacked, and that look in Pitt's eyes before she bites Madeline Smith is sexual, pure and simple. The nude romps, which seemed more flashy and sensational back in 1970, today seem more carefully crafted to demonstrate the seductive influence of evil, and how sexual seduction is similar to the seduction of evil. Ingrid Pitt, looking beautiful yet somehow infinitely sad and pale, almost haggard, captures the loneliness of the undead and demonstrates vampirism as both a sexual urge and also as a disease. Her performance resonates and grows richer over time. Here is not the typical Hammer Glamour model who frolics in the nude, for Pitt, though quite beautiful with a well proportioned body, was exotic and mature in a way that separates her from most of the other female fashion queens. For Pitt truly submits a multi-layered performance here. While *The Vampire Lovers* offers one beheading too many, its vampiric violence and well-filmed cinematographic atmosphere create a movie several cuts above the other typical Hammer productions of that time.

Each movie features audio commentary with Ingrid Pitt and each film's respective director and screenwriter. Also included are original theatrical trailers and Ingrid Pitt reading sections from *Carmilla*, the original story on which *The Vampire Lovers* was based. Both films, made in 1970, showcase a rare European talent first emerging as the new star of Hammer horror. *Countess Dracula* and *The Vampire Lovers* have never appeared more complete or looked better. For anyone who thought these new movies were disposable, now is the time for serious re-evaluation.

The Ghoul
[MGM DVD]
Movie: 2.5; Disc: 3.5

People were shocked when, over the course of the last few years, 70 years of cobwebs, deterioration and inferior release prints were replaced by digitally corrected and restored DVD releases of many of the Universal horror classics. But even that cannot prepare the aficionado for the magnificent restoration that occurred with the seldom-seen British chiller of 1933, *The Ghoul*, starring horror film icon Boris Karloff. For years and years, all existing prints (16mm and VHS home video) of *The Ghoul* have been inferior, boasting light contrast and a third generation duped look. However, back in the 1970s and 1980s, we were told to be glad for any existing source material, for *The Ghoul* was virtually lost and this was the best we would ever get.

Now, for a realistic sell-through price of $10, MGM has released a pristine fine-grain print of *The Ghoul* looking better than it has looked since its original release 70 years ago. This lackluster release (from the promotional aspect) deserves to be shouted from marquee rooftops across the land, and it very well may be the most important release for classic horror movie fans this year.

The Ghoul, which at last can be fairly evaluated, is never better than 2.5 to perhaps 3.0 stars (fair to good at best), yet it features one of the finest horror movie casts (Karloff, Ernest Thesiger, Ralph Richardson and Cedric Hardwicke) and Karloff's performance is eerily interesting. Surprisingly his portrayal of Egyptologist Dr. Morlant is robust,

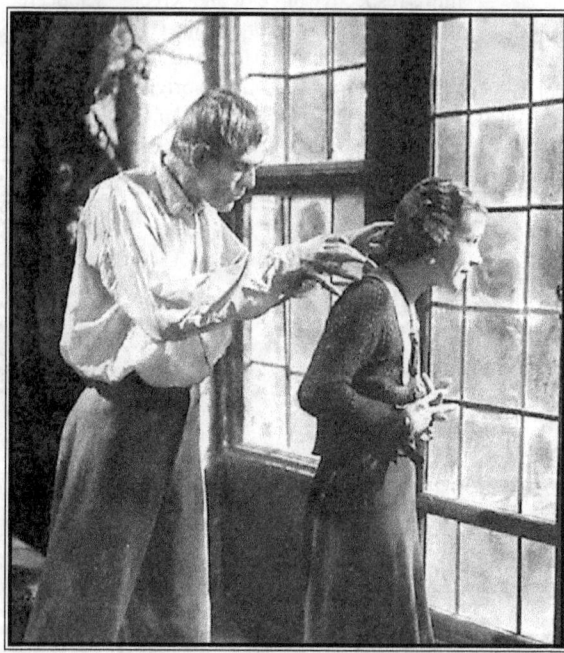

even if he plays a dying man at the film's beginning and reanimates from the dead as a living corpse for the remainder of the movie. It is odd that Karloff's deathbed sequence features the wearing of makeup that makes Karloff resemble a corpse even before he dies, and he doesn't look any different after death claims him.

Karloff delivers some spectacular sequences, especially when he is outside in the rain eying up Ernest Thesiger who is lurking in the cellar. With maniacal zeal, Karloff smashes the glass window and bends the metal bars protecting the home from intruders, easily squeezing through and stalking the terrified Thesiger. The cinematography illustrating Karloff's energetic corpse roaming about the old dark house is the stuff of which classic horror is made, but perhaps the most visually interesting sequence is the one where Karloff bows down to the Egyptian god who is supposed to open her hands to offer Karloff everlasting immortality. In the creepy sequence this does occur, but suddenly the viewer sees that the outstretched statue's hands have been replaced with human ones who snatch the immortality-bearing gemstone. A very visually mesmerizing sequence suggests the subtlety of Karl Freund's *The Mummy*, made one year earlier.

While this old dark house mystery variation of *The Mummy* with its focus on life after death is pedestrian in most ways, Karloff's contribution makes it something extra special. *The Ghoul* won't bump any of your top-20 horror classics from the list, but it is somehow refreshing to see such a landmark restoration of an almost lost horror classic hit the American shores in the fall of 2003. Rediscovering old chestnuts is what it's all about, and *The Ghoul* is one of the most important finds in many a year. Too bad no extras are included, but with a print looking and sounding (the film's sound, with full dynamic range, is almost equal to the superior visual appeal) this good, who needs the extras?

**The Haunted Palace
Tower of London**
[MGM Midnite Movies DVD]
Movie: [*Palace* 3.0; *Tower* 3.0];
Disc: 3.5

Here we have a double-bill of two fine movies that have unfairly become the bastard children of seemingly better productions. First, we have Roger Corman's 1963 production of H.P. Lovecraft's *Strange Case of Charles Dexter Ward,* released as *The Haunted Palace,* based upon a poem by Edgar Allan Poe to tie in with the successful Poe series. While *The Haunted Palace* is inferior to such superior Poe efforts as *The Fall of the House of Usher* and *Pit and the Pendulum,* it is nonetheless a horror movie of merit featuring one of Vincent Price's finest performances. And on the flip side of the DVD, we have Gene Corman's production of *Tower of London* (also directed by brother Roger), a low-budget 1962 remake of the 1939 Universal classic, but a movie that goes beyond the historical costume drama of the Universal original to evoke a ghastly sense of horror as low-rent *Macbeth.* Both of these films never garnered the credit they deserve, so what might appear to be one of the lesser releases in the MGM Midnight Movie series might very well become its shining jewel.

The Haunted Palace, once again demonstrating Roger Corman's artistry using Gothic Pathe color and the Panavision widescreen pallet, is an eerie chiller whose plot becomes secondary to its mood and vision. Using the frame of films such as *Black Sunday* and *City of the Dead/Horror Hotel,* the film begins over 100 years in the past as warlock Joseph Curwen (Vincent Price) is burned alive for his quest to mate human beings with mutated creatures to allow the Old Gods to return to rule the Earth. Like *Fall of the House of Usher,* Curwen's palace (moved to New England, stone by stone, from Europe) becomes a central character, his demonic portrait hanging over the fireplace becoming the symbol of evil that drives the movie. Curwen's heir, the identical looking Charles Dexter Ward (again played by Price), inherits his ancestral home and is immediately possessed by the spirit of Curwen who gains dominance over Ward via the evil portrait and its hypnotic influence. Vincent Price winningly executes a dual role segueing between the kindly and frightened Ward and the possessed and totally evil Curwen. It is truly one of Price's finest performances. The manner in which the timber of his voice changes, along with the intensity of his stare and the curl of his mouth, subtly conveys a powerful duality. Ward is saved from the burning castle at film's end and he rests against the very tree where his ancestor was most likely burned a century ago. Suddenly he turns around, a slight smile on his face, perhaps even an arrogant sneer, and the audience realizes that Ward has most likely been possessed by his demon ancestor once again and for the final time.

Add to this pivotal Price *tour de force* is Lon Chaney, submitting a fine supporting performance as Simon, where he creates a character similar to that of Klove, Count Dracula's dedicated manservant, in the middle-period Hammer Dracula movies. Chaney, looking healthier and in far fuller command of his faculties than he would appear a scant few years later, creates an eerie aura and makes two startling entrances during the course of the movie. Also, Elisha Cook does a wonderful turn in dual supporting parts. Debra Paget is quietly intense as Ward's concerned

wife who appears totally in the dark throughout all the horrible proceedings.

The Haunted Palace's script, written by Charles Beaumont, is a might too sketchy and underwritten, but the cinematography and mood and Vincent Price's performance all add up to a solid horror chiller that stands the test of time.

For me, the almost forgotten 1962 *Tower of London* is more entertaining and creates a better Gothic canvas than does the larger production of Universal's 1939 historical drama starring Basil Rathbone and Boris Karloff. In the Gene Corman produced and Roger Corman directed United Artists release, Vincent Price crafts a monstrous performance of hunchbacked Richard III as influenced by Shakespeare's *Hamlet* (Richard is always seeing ghosts who prompt him to action) and *Macbeth* (his bloodthirsty quest for power at all costs). This bargain basement Shakespeare reveals the Gothic and ghostly subplots that always inherited Shakepeare's plays (he was one to always please the masses). So we have a beardless Price (looking remarkably different than he does one year later in *The Haunted Palace*) murder his brother by stabbing him in the back and sliding the body into a vat of wine less than 10 minutes into the production. When an innocent woman refuses to help Richard renounce the birthright of the dead king's two sons, she is severely whipped and stretched on the rack until she dies, amid ghastly screams. When her ghost returns, sensually mocking Richard's deformities, she works him up into a rage so that when his wife Ann enters the room, he strangles his own wife, believing he is choking the ghost. In another cinema moment of derring-do, Richard and his henchman, played by Michael Pate, use pillows to suffocate the royal heirs, young children in their beds. We know that Hollywood frowns upon the murder of children, and the sequence is ghastly. Throughout the proceedings, Richard visits with the ghosts of his murder victims who taunt and threaten him, allowing Price to essay a slightly over-the-top performance that is surprisingly rich and always fun. This is the type of performance that Vincent Price is so wonderful at creating and why he is such a popular icon performer of horror cinema.

Perhaps Vincent Price is best in his coronation sequence where the archbishop is reluctant to perform the religious ceremony, so Richard puts on the robes and crown and carries his scepter to the open window where he proudly appears before his citizenry. At first Richard imagines hearing cheers and applause and smiles broadly, but soon he hears boos and shouts of disdain, and he pulls back inside. Because of the low-budget, the entire sequence is photographed tight on Price's face with his vanity and pride disintegrating into shock and dismay—we never see the hordes of crowds assembled, and to be truthful, all the noise Richard hears might only be a product of his own mind. But as directed by Roger Corman, the sequence picks up power because of (not in spite of) its bargain basement budget.

Simply stated, *Tower of London* is a delight and features a Shakespearean and even Dickensian influence, merging historical cinema with cinematic hauntings and the horror genre in a much more rewarding manner than the 1939 original could ever hope to achieve.

As is true with MGM DVD, both prints are absolutely gorgeous, with *The Haunted Palace* anamorphically enhanced for 16:9 monitors; however, the non-enhanced *Tower of London* (shot in crisp black and white) is only slightly letterboxed framed, so the resolution is strong. Also, each film features documentaries (filmed especially for the DVD release) with Roger and Gene Corman talking about the production of each movie. For a $15.00 list price, this double-feature package is a bargain.

**The Blood of Fu Manchu
(aka Kiss and Kill)**
[Blue Underground]
Movie: 2.0; Disc: 3.0

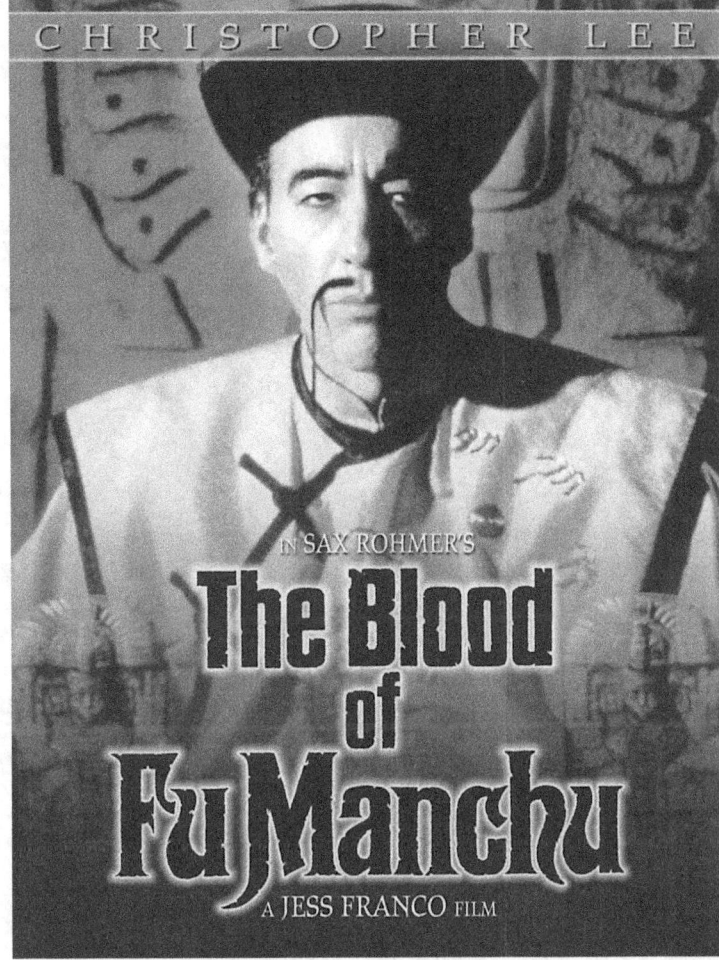

Christopher Lee always complained that the chief problem with the Hammer Film Production *Dracula* series was the simple fact that Hammer did not do Stoker, that they failed to portray the character as envisioned by the author. After doing the first two *Dracula* films, the ones directed by Terence Fisher, Lee always maintained that he did the others because he was blackmailed with the threat of putting loads of people out of work if he refused to do the production (which had already been presold with Lee's name). However, after the at-best good *Face of Fu Manchu*, the series rapidly deteriorated into a sorrowful state that made *Taste the Blood of Dracula* look like a classic. For instance, *The Blood of Fu Manchu*, released in 1968, contained very little style and even less charm. Director Jess Franco's penchant for quirky sex and nudity does not see much light of day here (yes, 10 women are chained and imprisoned in various stages of undress, and yes, a snake does nip at an exposed breast or two); however, Blue Underground must be praised for releasing a pristine widescreen print that is uncensored containing these flashes of nudity that never made the initial American release.

But with a cast featuring Christopher Lee as Fu, Shirley Eaton as one of the viper death squad, Richard Greene as Nayland Smith (who is blinded early on and spends most of the movie too weak to do much of anything) and Tsai Chin as Fu's daughter, the performances appear to have been phoned in. Christopher Lee, who looks imposing as Fu Manchu, has little to do except stand around unemotionally and bark orders. He literally does not blink an eye.

And putting Fu Manchu in South America and turning the film into a jungle programmer is deadly dull, at least when compared to the James Bond-ish antics of having the insidious Fu and his band of henchman invade the village green of jolly old England in the debuting Fu Manchu entry. Fu Manchu's operations transformed into the jungle just wreaks of budget constraints and makes the production unable to create Gothic chills and a menacing mood. The premise of having 10 luscious women filled to the brim with Cobra snake venom, making the kiss from each beauty deadly and ultimately fatal, is a good premise. But too much time is wasted having the women chained and bound in the jungle with Fu planning to eliminate his 10 most hated enemies.

Basically *The Blood of Fu Manchu* is a tedious programmer with little to offer except a gorgeous presentation. Extras include recent onscreen interviews with Christopher Lee, Jess Franco, producer/writer Harry Alan Towers and stars Tsai Chin and Shirley Eaton. These forums are worth the price of admission. Other extras include talent bios, trailers, poster and still gallery and the facts of Fu Manchu. Blue Underground offers quite an impressive package for a less than stellar movie. But as part of the four-film Christopher Lee Collection boxed set, the movie is worth a look.

The Hills Have Eyes
[Anchor Bay Entertainment]
Movie: 3.0; Disc: 4.0

Wes Craven's second film helped define the 1970s horror film, making this era in horror cinema distinct and easily identified. *The Hills Have Eyes*, almost too artistic a title for a low-budget drive-in style movie, stands with *The Texas Chain Saw Massacre*, *Deep Red* and *Halloween* as definitive horror classics of their era. The film was one of the first (along with David Cronenberg's *The Brood* and Sean Cunningham's *Last House on the Left*) to deal with the destruction of the American nuclear family. In the movie we have the extended Carter family off on a vacation traveling through the American southwest on their way to California (attempting to sneak over the border). In the rocky desert they encounter a feral, cannibalistic family of savages—inbred, deformed and mentally retarded—who are out to destroy America's finest. Interestingly, at first the primitive invaders only appear to be looking for food, which Pluto (Michael Berryman) steals when he first enters the camper. However, soon Mars (Lance Gordon) attacks and rapes the youngest daughter of the family and steals the infant child of oldest daughter (Dee Wallace). Along the way father Big Bob Carter (Russ Grieve) is set afire in the desert, mother Ethel (Virginia Vincent) is shot in the stomach and dies slowly over the course of the evening and Lynne dies trying to save her baby. The traditional family takes on the feral family, all fighting over the possession of the baby (who is to become a special meal for the cannibals). In order to live, the human survivors have to mimic the savage actions of their animalistic counterparts, the film ending on a freeze frame as hero Bobby (Robert Houston) savagely stabs Mars to death. In the final moments of the film, with the traditional family members viciously fighting back, the fine line between Christian family (who join hands at one point and pray standing in the desert) and feral one is blurred.

Unfortunately, *The Hills Have Eyes* is dated by its low-budget 1970s look, even though the relentless pacing and surprise shocks still manage to create malaise throughout. We have the clever use of the two dogs—Beauty and Beast—who represent the two extremes, with Beauty being savagely gutted early on, and soul-mate Beast becoming the avenging angel later in the movie (showing that the "beast" must emerge in order for survival to occur).

The two-disc set contains some fascinating extras, including two documentaries, one featuring interviews with the surviving cast, and the second highlighting all the films of Wes Craven. Both shorts are exceptional. We have one alternative ending (which re-edits an earlier sequence placing it at the end, with additional footage creating a more normal "everything-is-okay" ending). And finally we have poster and still gallery, trailers and bios. And best of all, *The Hills Has Eyes* has been remastered with a beautiful widescreen 16:9 enhanced print with sound remixed with DTS 6.1 or Dolby Digital 5.1 EX. The film has never looked nor sounded this good. While time has diminished the impact of the movie, *The Hills Have Eyes* still packs a visceral gut punch and features the ritualistic slaughter of a family for which we care a great deal. Wes Craven's second feature is one that still frightens audiences today.

LON CHANEY COLLECTION:
The Ace of Hearts;
Laugh, Clown, Laugh;
The Unknown;
London After Midnight;
Lon Chaney: A Thousand Faces
[Warner Home Video;
TCM Archives]
Movies: 3.0; Disc: 4.0

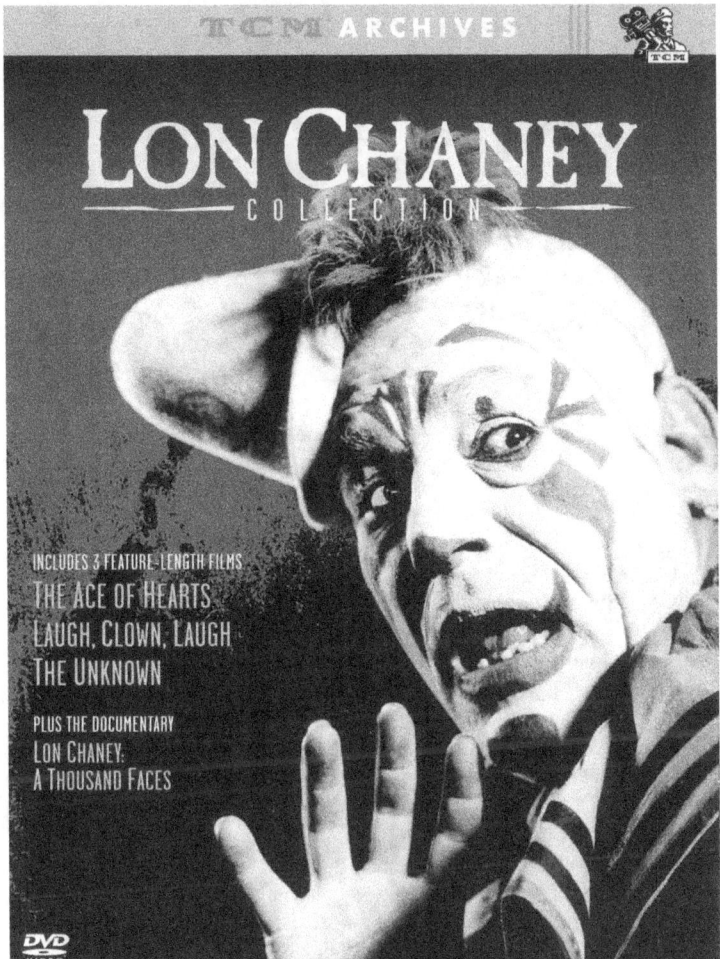

Thanks to the DVD medium, forgotten and sometimes lost silent films are being photographically reconstructed, restored and rescored. In the pages of the immortal magazine, *Famous Monsters of Filmland*, editor Forrest J Ackerman started the mantra "Lon Chaney Shall Not Die!" And while Chaney's films were almost forgotten back in the late 1950s, today in the zeroes his films are more accessible than ever before.

Turner Classic Movies and Warner Home Video have done a great service to classic movie lovers by lovingly reconstructing four of Chaney's movies (one, the long lost *London After Midnight*, has been reconstructed from available photos using an actual script of the movie and is almost utterly pointless). Also included is a 2000 documentary about the film career of Lon Chaney. The films receive insightful commentary by Lon Chaney historian Michael F. Blake and feature photo galleries. The terrific gatefold package unfolds to reveal two discs with delightful photos and graphics appearing on both the gatefold packaging, as well as the slipcase, giving the movies a deluxe treatment they most definitely deserve.

As host Robert Osborne reminds us, these Chaney movies explore the theme of unrequited love in all its perversities. In fact, these three movies (let us remove *London After Midnight* to the level of curiosity, as its presentation is hampered by the lack of stills used, with the camera zooming in or out of the same photos, which produces tedium after about 45 minutes) are eccentric, cutting edge delights revealing Lon Chaney not to be a horror icon, in the gist of a Boris Karloff or a Bela Lugosi, but an obsessive oddball in the sense of someone who might appear in a David Lynch production today. Chaney is not horrific as much as he is insidious, quirky or obsessed.

Theses traits are quickly evident in Chaney's performance in *The Ace of Hearts* (1921), the oldest film appearing in this collection. While the print features some lines that come and go and lots of speckling which produces a snowy look, overall the print remains sharp and clear with good contrast. The newly composed contest-winning score is also quite compatible with the film's tone—keyboard driven with sound effects added quite appropriately. As the movie opens, a group of men are meeting to decide the fate of a man guilty of "unscrupulous ambition on a colossal scale. Death would rid the world of such a menace." Chaney, playing a portrait painter, is one of the group who stands to seal the man's fate—death! These men will draw cards, and the one who gets the ace of hearts will be the assassin. Lillith, the only woman in the group, seems to be in love with the handsome man chosen as assassin; however, Lon Chaney's character secretly loves her from afar, and cut-aways reveal the sense of his passionate obsession to win her heart. In a very Hitchcockian sequence, the assassin becomes a waiter at a fancy restaurant where young lovebirds are holding hands and playing footsy under the table, as the waiter plants a small explosive nearby. Stating Lillith corrupted him, the assassin returns with the explosive in his possession, unable to kill, especially when young lovers are so near. The movie progresses from this point. But those intense

Joan Crawford and Lon Chaney in *The Unknown*

shots of Lon Chaney pining away in the shadows, his face registering his dismay over being unable to win the heart of Lillith, becomes the hallmark of a wonderful performance.

Laugh, Clown, Laugh, released in 1928, features a dense 35mm print with no speckling and some superficial scratching. A teenaged Loretta Young stars as the abandoned child taken in by circus clown Lon Chaney who raises her in the world of the circus. Showing that silent movies can be as weird as modern movies, *Laugh, Clown, Laugh* shows a truly depressed Lon Chaney (depressed because he loves his adopted daughter Simonetta and feels it would be inappropriate to express his physical desires) portraying an always-happy circus clown. While, for contrast, Count Ravelli has physical desires for Simonetta. She cuts her leg while climbing over barbed wire to fetch a flower on the Ravelli estate. The Count, all in the cause of prompt medical attention, takes the young girl up to his bedroom, yanks off her stocking and gently fondles her extended bare leg and foot. Fortunately, he is interrupted, which allows the young girl to escape. But the Count suffers from a nervous condition: bursts of uncontrollable laughter. The Count's doctor tells him that only by falling in love will he be cured. Thus, we have parallel contrasting characters with the morbidly depressed clown and the deliriously off-putting laughing Count. As Chaney's character reveals, he can make all of Rome laugh but he can never make himself laugh.

The third movie, *The Unknown*, released in 1927, features another sharp 35mm fine grain print with some lines that come and go. With a scenario worthy of David Lynch and other *avant garde* directors, *The Unknown* tells the story of armless knife-throwing circus performer Alonzo (Lon Chaney) who uses Nanon Zanzi (Joan Crawford) as his sexy assistant, the provocative woman who strikes sensual poses on a spinning platform after she sheds most of her clothing. Of course Alonzo has desires for her, but she has a deep psychological fear of men, having always been pawed by frisky males causing her to shrink with fear when she thinks of men touching her. Alonzo, always near, swears "no one will get her but me." You see, Chaney's character is never a threat since he has no arms and throws his knives with his feet. However, early on, after taking a beating from Zanzi (Nick De Ruiz), Nanon's father, Alonzo and his dwarf assistant Cojo (John George) pay a visit to Zanzi's wagon, when Alonzo gleefully drops his cape to Zanzi and reveals he does possess arms (using a harness, he has them strapped to his body during the day to win the sympathy of Nanon), which he gleefully uses when he bends over and slowly extends his massive hands closer to Zanzi's neck. From the wagon a horrified Nanon sees the murder, except the murderer's back is facing her and all she can really see is those murderous hands. Once again, Lon Chaney appears bold and masculine at times, yet when Nanon hurts his feelings, his face erupts into a baleful of tears. And considering that his quirky character is placed within such an offbeat plot, *The Unknown* becomes one of the strangest movies ever produced.

When we consider these three features plus the addition of the photo-restored *London After Midnight* and the Chaney documentary, the Lon Chaney Collection becomes a treasure trove of lost cinema carefully restored to its absolute finest visual quality. With the addition of audio commentaries and photo galleries, the collection becomes one of the top-10 DVD releases of the past year, absolutely essential for fans of Lon Chaney, silent cinema and the offbeat.

Dr. Jekyll and Mr. Hyde (1932)
Dr. Jekyll and Mr. Hyde (1941)
[Warner Home Video]
Movie (1932: 3.5; 1941: 3.0);
Disc: 3.5

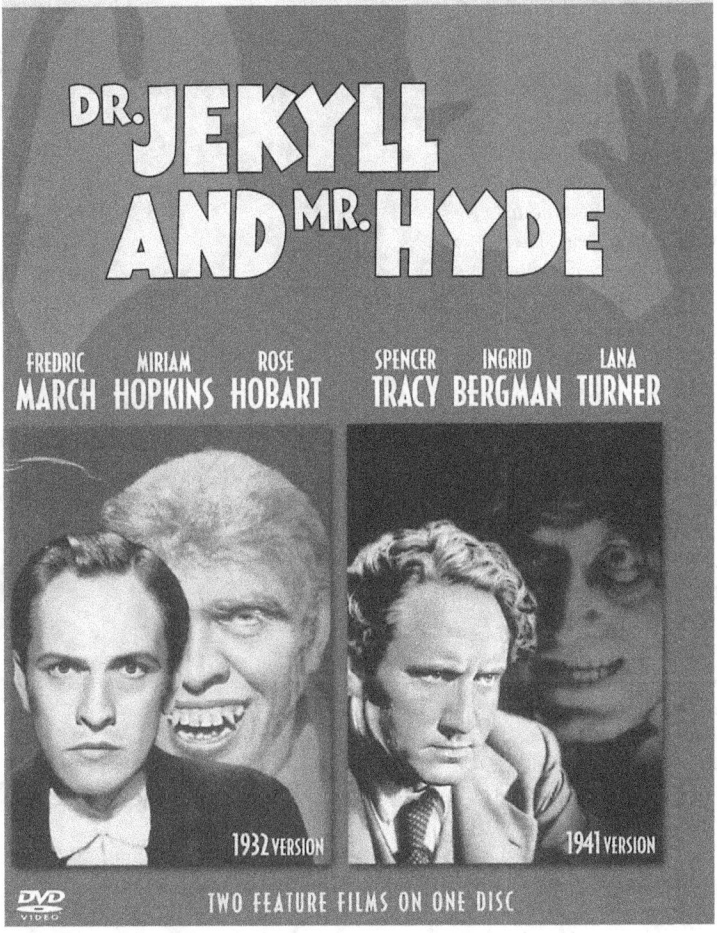

Amazing, only a few days into 2004 and one of the most important DVD collections of the year was released, a budget-priced double-feature of both the Fredric March and Spencer Tracy versions of *Dr. Jekyll and Mr. Hyde*, two important horror classics from the early 1930s and 1940s.

The most lauded version, the 1932 Rouben Mamoulian-directed version that stars Fredric March (who was co-winner for Best Actor at the Academy Awards for his performance as Jekyll and Hyde) is perhaps the greatest non-Universal horror classic of the 1930s. Even though sound cinema was still in its infancy, Mamoulian amplifies every grasp as Jekyll transforms into monstrous Hyde, emphasizes every bubbling beaker in his laboratory and sometimes allows the sound of a broken cane smashing the human skull to graphically depict grisly murders. Mamoulian innovatively starts off his movie with a subjective sequence allowing the movie audience to become Jekyll, the audience seeing its own face when the good doctor glances into a mirror. Later, when Jekyll first transforms into Hyde, the audience again watches the sequence subjectively with our own cinematic hands mixing the chemicals and gulping them down.

What makes this version of Jekyll and Hyde a classic horror movie is the fact that Hyde is a primitive, simian version of earlier man, stripped of his social consciousness allowing the beast to dominate. Basically, the movie is a were-ape tale where a decent human being transforms into his primordial pre-civilized self, first induced by chemicals, but soon induced by the simple power of mind over matter as the beast gains control over the rational human.

March as Hyde is breathtaking in a landmark performance that still rivets audiences today. When the ape-man Hyde, wearing top hat and tails, goes into the rainy evening, looking skyward and opening his mouth to taste the rain, such a simple sequence sums up all our primitive pleasures. In the club sequence with Ivy (Miriam Hopkins) where Hyde attempts to woo her with his bottle of champagne and promise of money to be thrown her way, the sexually driven man whose self-imposed sense of power fuels his libido becomes classic cinema. Contrasted is the earlier sequence where the not-so-innocent Jekyll comes to Ivy's aide taking her home and putting her in bed. There she playfully strips for the good doctor, plants kisses on his lips and dangles her naked leg from underneath her flimsy covers and moans "Come back soon!" Jekyll, quite physically interested, is interrupted by good friend Lanyon (Holmes Herbert) who reminds him of his decency. However, the doctor's sexual longing for the desirable lower-class tart comes to the surface in the guise of Mr. Hyde.

Rose Hobart is unfortunately bland as good-girl Muriel Carew, Jekyll's fiancée. The polite young thing is bound by the dictates of her oppressive society, as represented by her father. Equally bland and stiff is Fredric March as Jekyll, who delivers lines such as "This is my penance" as he announces to God, looking skyward, that he will give up the love of his life in order to maintain his humanity. Whereas as Hyde, March exudes delirious energy in a performance that literally twitches, Jekyll's every line seems overly rehearsed, deliberate and theatrical. But March's Hyde joins the ranks of icon horror film performances and every sequence in which Hyde appears is a classic one.

This Mamoulian 1932 Paramount classic almost disappeared when MGM decided to remake the Paramount version nine years later. Hoping to avoid comparisons between the two productions, MGM attempted to buy the rights to the earlier production so they could destroy prints and make their own version of *Dr. Jekyll and Mr. Hyde* the definitive version. In this version Spencer Tracy portrays the dual roles with luscious cinematic sex symbols Ingrid Bergman (as Ivy) and Lana Turner (as fiancée Beatrix) as the female love/sex interest. In this Victor Fleming-directed production, Bergman and Turner are interestingly cast against type with Bergman playing the lower-class floozy who attempts to seduce the good doctor and usual femme fatale Turner playing the socially acceptable demure bride-to-be of Jekyll. While Mamoulian's movie was cast as hardcore horror with the emphasis on Jekyll's transformation into the simian Hyde, nine years later the Fleming version seems more Hollywood mainstream and focuses on Freudian suspense and romance (let's face it, Miriam Hopkins was sexual from the neck down but she was no classic beauty), courtesy of Turner and Bergman, two of Hollywood's sizzling female stars of the era. The movie's most innovative sequences involve brief Freudian dream/visions as Jekyll transforms into Hyde. Sequences of the two females smiling seductively overtly tempting the socially acceptable Jekyll into sexual

merriment is best symbolized by the sequence of Jekyll gleefully riding a white horse and fiercely whipping the poor beast to run faster, a delirious look on Hyde's face. When suddenly, in the dream, the horse morphs into the naked head and shoulders of Bergman and Turner. While such dream sequences are short, they are visually tantalizing and symbolic of the raging desires bubbling just below Jekyll's surface (or stirring just below the waist).

Spencer Tracy's Dr. Jekyll, becoming a more complex character than March was ever allowed to be back in 1932, is passionate about medical science being a business of risk taking and self-sacrifice and he gallantly decides to put his life on the line to advance knowledge. Tracy, squat and not conventionally handsome (at least when compared to March), becomes a figure of passion and commitment. However, his Edward Hyde is subtle and almost ordinary looking. Just as March's Hyde progressively deteriorated and became uglier with each transformation, Tracy's initial transformations make him look different, perhaps bedheaded and wild-eyed but definitely not monstrous. Even at the end of the movie, his Hyde develops bags beneath his eyes, his eyebrows grow wild and bushy and his hair becomes messy, but no one would mistake him for a gorilla in top hat and tails. While audiences wish for Tracy's Hyde to become monstrous and bestial, his transformation is one of internal characterization based more upon acting than makeup. While both approaches are valid, I prefer March's monster portrayal over Tracy's human degenerate approach, so while March earns my attention for his Hyde, Tracy wins me over with his multi-layered performance as Jekyll.

Both prints feature pristine fine-grain 35mm prints (the 1932 is slightly rough, but considering the fact that this film was once lost, the DVD version is the absolute best I have ever seen) with the 1941 Tracy version being close to pristine. Extras include a beautiful looking Warner Bros. Bugs Bunny cartoon, *Hyde and Hare*, a trailer of the 1941 film and audio commentary of the 1932 version by Midnight Marquee staff writer Greg Mank (whose theatrical background makes his commentary dramatic and insightful).

When it comes to essential DVDs for the horror movie buff, this double feature is a must-have.

Shivers
(aka They Came from Within)
[Image Entertainment]
Movie: 2.5; Disc: 3.0

David Cronenberg was much more fun when he began his feature film career as a horror film director who made *Shivers* (retitled *They Came From Within* by American International for US release) in 1975. When released in the US, the MPAA forced AIP to trim the release print to get an R rating and so Americans never saw the uncut director's print of the movie, until now.

Right at the dawning of sexual conservatism with the emergence of AIDS a few years off and other blood-borne sexually transmitted diseases slowly gaining publicity, *Shivers* details the end of the Age of Aquarius and the sexually promiscuous lifestyles promoting orgies, swinging and wife swapping. In this exploitative gem, a scientist uses a sexually active young woman to create a phallic (of course!) parasite that eliminates all sexual inhibitions. She infects several people living in a newly opened Canadian high rise apartment complex, and for the rest of the movie, the sexual acrobatics between male and female (and female and female and male and male) escalate until this modern plague finally hops into automobiles and threatens to infect all of Canada.

Of course this film depicts such an epidemic not as a softcore sex movie might but as an exploitative horror movie 1970s-style, with a male host existing in semi-zombie state throughout the movie, the phallic pet slithering out of his mouth and back in again, the parasite writhing slightly under the skin wiggling across his abdomen. Sexual predators force themselves on unwary victims, climaxing by transferring the parasite from themselves to their newly initiated victims orally. Once infected, humans become zombified hosts for their parasite and resemble a product of the George Romero school of filmmaking. Even horror cult actress Barbara Steele has a cameo as Betts, portraying a lesbian ready to exit her closet (or in this case, bathtub).

As seen today, *Shivers* has lost a lot of its edge and surprise; however, David Cronenberg's direction is still devilishly claustrophobic (getting the most out of his swinging apartment complex) and features shock upon shock, delivered in his typical gooey biological manner. Perennial Cronenberg actor Joe Silver delivers an effective supporting role, and heroine Lynn Lowry submits a heroin-chic performance that resembles the similar turn committed by Dana Wynter in the original *Invasion of the Body Snatchers*. Lowry seems to have been selected for her parasite-infected performance, which is outstanding, contrasted to her generic pretty heroine performance.

Extras include an onscreen interview with David Cronenberg and a trailer. While *Shivers* was innovative and cutting edge back in 1975, today, almost 30 years later, it reveals an uninhibited, non-pretentious David Cronenberg directing one of the best exploitative horror films of the decade, one that still holds up pretty well.

The Devil Commands
[Columbia Home Video]
Movie: 3.0; Disc: 3.0

Back in 1941, Boris Karloff was about to conclude what has come to be known as his four Columbia Mad Doctor pictures; the best remains *The Devil Commands*, here rendered in a sharply focused fine-grain black and white 35mm print. Of course a few lines and scratches surface here and there, but the print is simply outstanding. Director Edward Dmytryk, still directing B programmers, was on the brink of an outstanding motion picture career (*The Caine Mutiny, Murder My Sweet, Raintree County*). So we have Boris Karloff in a performance that is both sympathetic and monstrous (and he's on screen in almost every sequence) working with a first-rate director in a tight 65-

minute B production that thoroughly entertains.

The film opens in noirish voice-over fashion, and ends the same way, with a moody shot of a spooky old home out in the country. Karloff begins the movie with slicked-to-the-side dark hair, portraying a respected science department chair of the local college whose research (communication using thought projection and brain waves) upsets his university peers. In a gut-wrenching sequence, Karloff's wife dies tragically in a car accident, Karloff's spirit dying with her. Now his research turns to contacting the dead, and after hooking up with a fake spiritualist, a very domineering woman Mrs. Walters (Anne Revere in one of the strongest female horror film performances of the 1940s), he ignores his grieving daughter and surfaces two years later, now with dour expression and graying hair that is demonically frizzy and wild. His laboratory is unlike any lab in horror film history, with corpses seated around a table with metal helmets around their heads, which, when activated, create a whirlwind of tornado activity causing the stiffs to lean inward toward the center of the table. For a low-budget, such special effects, aided immeasurably by the storm-within-the-lab sounds, are quite effective.

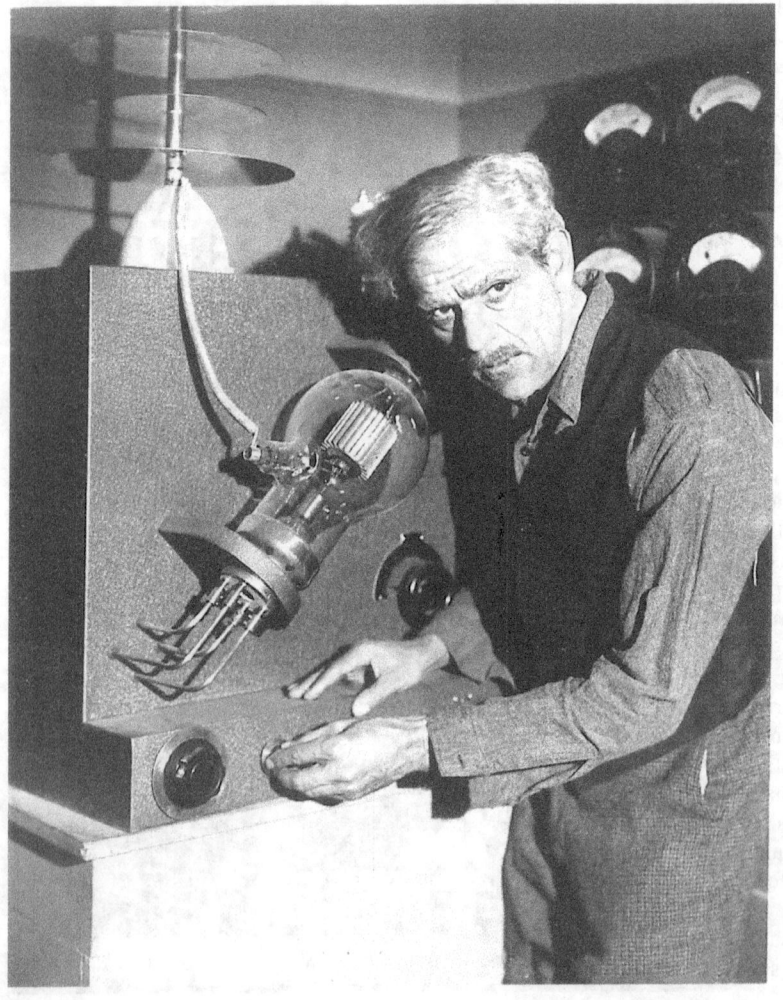

Interestingly, Boris Karloff's performance runs the gamut of emotions from dutiful father and husband to obsessive scientist, grieving widower, to victim of his experiments, to emotionally vacant and heartless automaton. For a B production, Karloff dares to convey the heightened emotions that Bela Lugosi always gets credit for creating. It is definitely one of Karloff's finest 1940s performances, and the film more than holds up its end (its sometimes too abrupt ending only channels the theme that humans that invade God's turf are doomed to sudden destruction). No extras are included, but the beautiful print and the chance that the other three entries in the series may see release gives us grounds for hope!

Near Dark
[Anchor Bay Entertainment]
Movie: 3.0; Disc: 4.0

After Hammer and Universal created the legendary cinematic vampire mythos, it took the influence of Euro Horror in the 1960s through the 1980s to subvert and reinvent such mythology by injecting a healthy diet of perverted sexuality, deemphasizing the religious significance and once again making vampirism a disease, both of the body and of the spirit. By the 1970s and 1980s, Hollywood was ready to revisit vampirism, not by exploring the past, but by forging ahead.

Kathryn Bigelow's low-budget 1987 release, *Near Dark*, can justly lay claim for being the most innovative vampire movie of the modern era, a movie that is dependent upon its outstanding ensemble cast of fine actors, three of which appeared together in *Aliens* (Lance Henriksen, Bill Paxton and Jenette Goldstein) a year earlier. If cinehistory were just, Lance Henriksen would have become the iconic horror actor of his generation, pushing aside franchise stunt men (all those who put on the hockey mask to play Jason or Robert Englund's kiss-your-ass-you're-so-lucky take on Freddy Krueger), and his performance as the Southern Confederate soldier surviving into modern times demonstrates exactly why. With his sharp aquiline facial features, his resounding deep bass voice and his intensity of performance getting under the skin of every character he undertakes, Henriksen had the talent, the passion and the dedication to become the modern-era Karloff, Lugosi, Cushing, Lee or Price. A shame that never worked out. Bill Paxton, playing the mean-spirited but good-looking cowboy, the man who knows how to use his spurs in a good bar fight, has the best lines to deliver, of course, all done in the modern era comic sense of "It's finger-licking good" after he feasts on human flesh and blood. Even pretty vampire Jenny Wright and hero Adrian Pasdar rise to the occasion by committing performances worthy of attention in any film genre.

Bigelow casts her entire film in nighttime sequences, or at most lights her environment in fading twilight or the cracking of dawn's early light. Her vampires are a blood cult family who kill for food but who seem to enjoy the kill as demonstration of their strength, their element of surprise and the true pleasure of bloodlust. Pasdar's Caleb, smitten with slutty, blonde beer-swilling Jenny Wright's Mae character, allows her to nibble on his neck, rendering him a member of the undead almost immediately. Vampirism as cast by Bigelow is akin to drug addiction, but the twist is the urge to kill, to feed, must overcome any previously learned system of morals. Caleb is given one week to make a kill, and for all that time all he can bring himself do is drain Mae's vein in her arm after she kills her victim. She warns him as he slurps up her lifeforce not to drink too much, or the loss of blood would kill her. Even when his life is on the line, he cannot kill and never does. He buys time by saving the cult from sudden death, but he ultimately takes the cure via blood transfusion, something Mae also does at the end after the cult has been destroyed (in perhaps a too splashy special effects sequence that cheapens the subtlety of the overall production).

This two disc THX mastered set (talk about gorgeous print with a wonderful surround soundtrack) features a second disc of extras, including currently filmed documentaries with the majority of the cast and crew, one deleted scene, trailers, storyboards, poster and art gallery, behind-the-scenes stills, talent bio, etc. *Near Dark* never looked nor sounded this good, and the extras alone make purchasing this DVD set essential. *Near Dark* is one of the true modern horror film classics, and while it remains flawed and is limited by its low budget, its world-weary script and outstanding performances make it one of the more interesting horror movies produced within the past 30 years.

Hercules in the Haunted World
[Fantoma Films]
Movie: 2.0; Disc: 3.0

Generally movie fans credit Mario Bava's 1960 production of *Black Sunday* with creating, for mainstream audiences, the black-and-white look of Euro Horror, a visual style that blends the Gothic denseness of 1930s Universal with Cocteau's *Beauty and the Beast*. The cinematography of *Black Sunday* is well worth the price of admission, but the film offers much more. Three years later Bava returned with *Black Sabbath*, a movie that demonstrated what Bava could concoct with color photography.

What most fans of Mario Bava forget is that the Italian director's second movie, *Hercules in the Center of the Earth* (released in America as *Hercules in the Haunted World*), produced in 1961, featured intense color photography that *Black Sabbath* would be credited for introducing. While *Black Sabbath* is the superior production by far, *Hercules in the Haunted World* is dazzling visually, highlighting CinemaScope photography dripping with deeply saturated Technicolor. Added to the mix is Christopher Lee's villainous turn as Lyco, an additional treat for horror movie fans.

The Fantoma DVD source material is exceptional, featuring the original uncut European version. Generally, when Technicolor prints are released to DVD they look slightly washed out and lose their intense dark hues. However, *Hercules in the Haunted World* comes very close to approximating the theatrical Technicolor look. The print can be viewed in both the Italian language version with English subtitles or as an American dubbed version. Neither version seems to be superior to the other as the plot is silly and the dubbing no more obtrusive than the subtitles.

Muscleman Reg Park plays a marvelous Hercules and his reliance on the gods returns the character to his mythological roots. The production, mostly setbound, was photographed by Bava as well as directed by him, so the studio-crafted world is totally Bavaesque and the cinematography and mood became the major (only?) strengths of the production. The movie's dominant visual sequences all command the audience's attention. In the beginning we have Lyco's treasure room where one man thinks he is going to be rewarded with twisted gold. However, the devious Lyco rewards the man with spring-triggered swords that burst from the walls impaling his unfortunate victim within the treasure chamber. Once Hercules and friend go to Hades, the visuals become mesmerizing with a gigantic rock man threatening to crush our hero, so Hercules boldly lifts the rock man over his head and smashes him against a wall of stone. Hercules' friend hangs by a thread over a river of molten lava until his strength gives out and he falls in. However, in Bava's vision of Hades, the man is rescued before his soul can be claimed, so he survives to live and love another day (and he may well be the most over-sexed second banana in movie history). But things get incredibly Bavaesque in Lyco's underground crypt during the movie's climax when demons and vampires rise from their tombs and horrify audiences until Lyco, who will gain immortality if he drinks the blood of Deianira, is finally laid to rest.

Hercules in the Haunted World doesn't make much sense, its plot is by the numbers sword-and-sandal, but the film becomes artistically audacious by the participation of Mario Bava as photographer and director. The creation of creatures of the night all set within the framework of Hades and underground catacombs makes this movie one of the most artistic examples of sword-and-sandal cinema. Perhaps *Hercules in the Haunted World* is minor Bava, but in the case of style becoming substance, the movie warrants a viewing or two.

The Man Who Changed His Mind
[Shanachie Entertainment]
Movie: 2.5; Disc: 3.5

Months after the rare Gaumont British film *The Ghoul* was restored and released on MGM DVD, we now have another seldom seen Gaumont British horror chiller starring Boris Karloff restored and released to DVD, *The Man Who Changed His Mind* (1936). And a relatively new DVD label, Shanachie, as part of its British Cinema Collection, has released the movie to little fanfare. The release sports a duo-tone photographic cover without any booklet insert, but the movie itself features a generally pristine 35mm print with excellent contrast and very good sharpness. The film's only flaw is a slighty hissy soundtrack that could have been cleaned up digitally, but the sound is still full-bodied.

Boris Karloff, in one of his first mad doctor performances as Dr. Laurience (perhaps *The Invisible Ray* a year earlier started the trend), portrays a solitary scientist who is working on a contraption that switches brains electronically from one person to another (no gloppy brains in beakers or the use of scalpel or brain surgery required), much as we might transfer data from our computer's hard drive to a backup hard drive system. While the tone of this stodgy Brit production (directed by Robert Stevenson) works against itself at times, Boris Karloff submits one of his best performances ever as a mad doctor. Sporting a full head of graying hair with a slightly stooped posture, always holding, sucking on or lighting a cigarette, a world-weary look of defeat always stamped on his face, Dr. Laurience surprisingly, especially for the time, invites a female scientist to join him in his research and medical experimentation because she is the only colleague open to new ideas.

After working solo in a dilapidated lab, Laurience is seduced by the offer of corporate sponsorship by journalist Lord Haselwood (Frank Cellier) who offers Laurience richer quarters for his research and whose son Dick is making a play for Laurience's female assistant, Clare (Anna Lee). Haselwood rushes things and forces Laurience to publish his research and present his radical medical research to a public audience that verbally mocks the recluse. Of course this public ridicule is the impetus needed to drive Laurinece off the deep end, causing him to

switch Lord Haselwood's brain with his patient/servant Clayton (Donald Calthrop) who earlier told Clare that he doesn't know what was worse, his miserable body or his perverted mind (the man is wheelchair bound, obviously a stroke victim with one side of his body partially paralyzed). Clayton's body dies during the experiment but not before laughing at the suggestion that Clayton makes, now in the seemingly fit body of Haselwood, that he at last inhabits a healthy body. In an ironic twist it is revealed that Haselwood is dying of heart disease and that Clayton's brain has literally jumped from the fat into the fire.

By the time of the chilling climax, Laurience in wild-eyed abandonment (with shadowy photography emphasizing the lisping delivery of dialogue) strangles the body of Lord Haselwood and makes sure he is seen by both servant and policeman leaving the Haselwood home, guaranteeing Laurience will be convicted of the journalist's murder. Laurience's scheme, in the meanwhile, is to switch his brain into Dick Haselwood's body, and switch Dick's brain into his own body, so Dick (in Laurience's body) will be executed for the murder of his father and Laurience (in Dick's body) will inherit Lord Haselwood's estate and fortune. In a weirdly imaginative performance during the climax, John Loder as Dick actually tries to imitate Karloff's Laurience with his clenched hand holding a cigarette and his stiff gait and full head of hair resembling the gestures of Karloff from earlier in the film. After a terrifying fall from the second floor window, the body of Laurience lies dying on the ground, but Clare is able to undo the brain switching experiment, thus returning Dick to Dick's body and Laurience to Laurience's body, just before the evil scientist dies recanting his research and ordering his lab destroyed by Clare.

The Man Who Changed His Mind lacks the twisted and audacious shenanigans inherent in both the Monogram, PRC and Columbia mad doc films featuring Karloff and Bela Lugosi, but Karloff's performance is nuanced and rises above the film's other limitations. Seldom seen, classic horror buffs may be inclined to over praise the production, but while the film is at best of journeyman quality, Karloff's performance makes *The Man Who Changed His Mind* one film worth returning to time and time again.

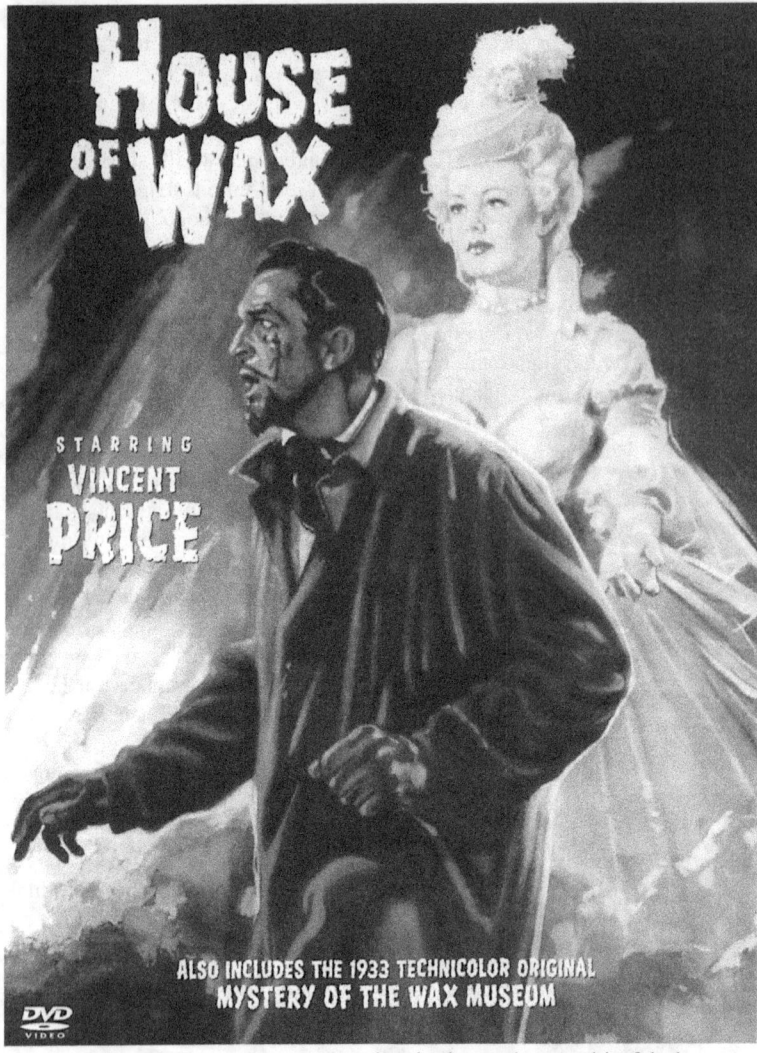

House of Wax
Mystery of the Wax Museum
[Warner Home Video] Movie
(*House*: 3.0; *Mystery*: 2.5);
Disc: 3.5

It made sense to double-bill Warner's *Doctor X* and *Mystery of the Wax Museum* on laserdisc a decade ago (both were early 1930s horror classics filmed in two-strip Technicolor and served as the Warner Bros. answer to Universal's horror film success), but it makes even more sense to double-bill *Mystery of the Wax Museum* and its remake *House of Wax* on DVD today. Bravo!

Even though revisionist criticism has of late favored the 1933 *Mystery of the Wax Museum*, upon subsequent viewings (such as watching both movies on this fabulous DVD double feature disc) it is apparent that 1953's *House of Wax* is the superior film.

Mystery of the Wax Museum looked more colorful on its laserdisc release, and I suspect that the restored master was overlooked for its DVD release (which does look sharper and boasts a full-bodied soundtrack). In some sequences, mostly darker ones, the deeply saturated color shines through, heavily accented toward blue tones. However, many sequences appear to be filmed in black and white (or a variation of sepia), which wasn't the case on laserdisc. However, it is Glenda Farrell's hard-as-nails reporter (the counterpart to Lee Tracy's similar role in *Doctor X*) that grates, especially her interaction with her editor with whom she reluctantly admits she has fallen in love. Farrell is feisty and fun, but her blonde hardness makes her difficult on the eyes and ears after a while. Original horror scream queen Fay Wray is her typical delightful self, but her role becomes secondary to Farrell's and Wray seems to have less to do here. Lionel Atwill, one of the premier villains of horror cinema, replaces his gruff British accent for a foreign one, and his attempt to be sympathetic undermines his aura of evil that he typically exudes. Atwill's monster makeup, a reptilian concept instead of a more

typical burn victim visage, rivals the hideousness of Fredric March's Mr. Hyde. Atwill is wonderful in such makeup, but he is mute except for the final climax and there his booming accent actually works against the horror of the face. Basically, the plot of both movies is virtually the same, but somehow the remake is better paced and holds viewer interest more consistently. *Mystery of the Wax Museum*, even when compared to the superior *Doctor X*, pales against most of the other 1930s horror heavy hitters, even the non-Universal ones, and while it is a solid horror programmer, it lacks the style and bite of the more formidable classics of the era.

House of Wax, made 20 years later, became a horror classic in the science fiction film era and its period detail makes the Andre de Toth WarnerColor/3-D film (the equivalent gimmick of its own time) an anomaly of its cinematic age. However, Vincent Price's performance as the sculptor/burn victim/madman is among Price's finest performances and the simple look of the film (both period set design and cinematography which makes full use of color photography) renders it superior to the original. The performances are stronger and bring the viewer more deeply into the plot: Carolyn Jones' blonde floozy who knows her own limitations and meets a tragic death; Phyllis Kirk's heroine who is always perky and loyal to her dead friend; Paul Picerni's dashing hero; Vincent Price's kindly then embittered artist who goes over the edge of sanity.

House of Wax succeeds based upon marvelous horrific sequences which are carefully paced throughout the production, never allowing attention to drift (not even the gimmicky paddle-ball man right after the Intermission [yes, the DVD features the Intermission title card]. We have the initial wax museum fire and explosion; the elevator shaft murder of Price's greedy partner; Kirk's finding Jones' corpse dead in bed, with the ghastly image of Price hiding in the shadows; the film's best sequence, the misty night street side chase of the black-cloaked Price pursuing Kirk through the fog; the morgue sequence where the disguised-as-a-corpse Price steals the body of Jones; Price's second attempt to sneak into Kirk's bedroom to kill her; the horrible images inside the wax museum; and the final confrontation between Kirk and Price where she cracks his mask and reveals the crippled artist to be the monstrous fiend.

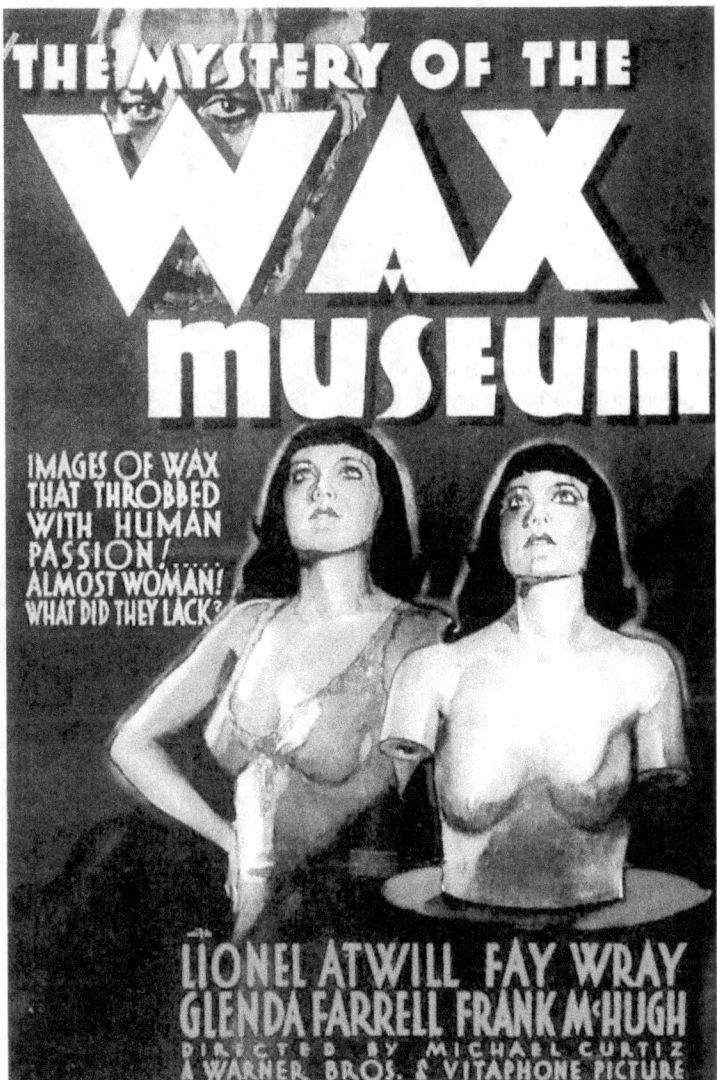

The movie is definitely mainstream Hollywood entertainment, a horror movie made for the masses, one that is never too frightening and one that is safe for the entire family. Despite this handicap, the film's pacing and storyline is fun and Vincent Price's performance, whether he is the cloaked monster sneaking through alleys and morgues or the kindly sculptor who instructs his disciple to make the clay sculpted mouth more cruel, is a delight. *House of Wax* is one of the finest American horror movies produced during the decade of the 1950s and it never looked so good on DVD. Extras include a trailer and newsreel footage showing the Hollywood premier of *House of Wax* (including Bela Lugosi's appearance with a man in an ape suit). Two quirky and fun movies for the price of one DVD... what better incentive to purchase both *Mystery of the Wax Museum* and *House of Wax*, two essential chillers to add to one's collection.

Captain Kronos: Vampire Hunter
[Paramount Home Video]
Movie: 2.5; Disc: 3.0

Hammer is hotter than ever, and now Paramount Home Video is coming through with budget-priced editions of two of the best latter-day Hammers, *Captain Kronos: Vampire Hunter* and *Frankenstein and the Monster from Hell*. Both widescreen DVD releases are enhanced for 16:9 monitors and are gorgeous prints, pristine quality with solid colors and sound. *Captain Kronos: Vampire Hunter*, unfortunately, does not contain any extras except for the wonderful audio commentary track presided over by Jonathan Sothcott and featuring writer/director Brian Clemons and cult actress Caroline Munro. However, when this movie can be found in Wal-Mart for $6, well, who can possibly complain?

By 1972 most of the familiar Hammer technical crew was gone… only editor James Needs stands out in the credits as being a member of the old guard. However, writer/director Brian Clemons had the vision of creating a new franchise hero, one very similar to Hugh Jackman's interpretation of *Van Helsing*. Here we have the physically dashing blond captain Kronos, unfortunately played by the slightly bland Horst Janson, who returns from war and finds his mother and sister vampirized. Miraculously surviving the vampire attacks, Kronos and his hunchbacked assistant devote their lives to eradicating the species, and the formula would have Kronos embarking upon a new vampire adventure each movie. Similar to a younger, sexier Errol Flynn-inspired version of Peter Cushing's Van Helsing… but unfortunately, Janson does not come close to capturing the charisma of the elder Cushing.

Clemons' vampire mythos is different, interesting, but while visually it does maintain interest, its logic and rationality leaves much to be desired. It seems the youthful victims of vampires are momentarily mesmerized by a figure in a black cloak, and within the blink of an eye (one vampire attack occurs while a roguish boyfriend waits in the woods and watches as his young girlfriend slowly walks out of the woods to her home; while the girl momentarily goes out of sight when walking down a slight slope, we hear giggling and then a scream, as the girl has already been attacked), the victims are still barely alive, having been sucked dry of energy and youth, left with a trickle of blood running down their lips (apparently these vampires bite on the lip so victims drip blood from the mouth, not their vampire attackers). Somehow such a mythos is not as erotic or visually impressive as the sight of a fanged male vampire burying his teeth into the soft neck flesh of the female victim.

As it turns out the vampires belong to an isolated aristocratic family, the Durwoods, presided over by an aging, bedridden mother and her two beautiful and young children (one played by Shane Briant). The one daughter refuses to look at the "old crone" because the thought of aging and looking ugly is repulsive to the beautiful woman. Ah, we now think we know the motivation of such vampire evil because we now understand the reasoning for the killings. However by film's end we see that old crone mother is actually wearing a mask and that she has brought her dead husband back from the dead to assist her in her vampire slayings, to restore her youth and beauty. The children, it is revealed, are totally innocent. So Clemons' script is full of surprises and he does attempt to imbue the story with twists of traditional vampire lore.

The lovely Caroline Munro, freed by Kronos from the stockades ("for dancing on Sunday"), becomes his immediate and willing mistress who stands by his side and even agrees to be the lure to attract the vampires at the film's climax. Munro's character is played for full sex appeal as she is given two sequences where she is nude (unfortunately cloaked by the night or by her full-bodied hair), as she becomes the captain's sex toy. After building a relationship and putting her life on the line for the captain and his assistant, at the movie's end Kronos quickly pushes her aside, wishes her well (a tear wells up in her eye) and Kronos and hunchback hurriedly ride off into the sunset. Very unsatisfying. *Captain Kronos: Vampire Hunter*, while not a classic Hammer in any sense of the word, is quite imaginative and filled with surprises.

Universal Home Video Legacy Collection
Frankenstein: The Legacy Collection
[*Frankenstein*: 4.0; *Bride of Frankenstein*: 4.0; *Son of Frankenstein*: 3.5; *Ghost of Frankenstein*: 3.0; *House of Frankenstein*: 3.0]

Dracula: The Legacy Collection
[*Dracula*: 4.0; Spanish language *Dracula*: 3.5; *Dracula's Daughter*: 3.0; *Son of Dracula*: 3.0; *House of Dracula*: 3.0

The Wolf Man: The Legacy Collection
[*The Wolf Man*: 3.0; *Werewolf of London*: 3.0; *Frankenstein Meets the Wolf Man*: 3.5; *She-Wolf of London*: 2.0]

Disc: 4.0

For fans of classic horror movies, these three box sets are to drool over. First, yes, all of these movies have been formerly available on DVD, all except *House of Dracula* (DVD premier), but I wanted to make the case that Universal monster collectors would do well by purchasing all three box sets.

First of all, let's discuss the packaging. True, we do not get individual poster art of each movie, but the title depictions of Frankenstein's Monster, The Wolf Man and Dracula are superb graphic designs. Each gatefold box easily slides out of the slipcase which features a transparent panel on the front that allows the dominant monster in the set to be seen, but the transparent panel has a spooky background setting into which the face of the monster is perfectly framed. Inside the slipcase is a one page glossy insert, one side advertising all three box sets, the other detailing (short description with cast and credits) all four or five films contained in each box set. Then we have the expensive looking gatefold DVD case, the front containing the cover monster painting and title, the back containing sepia photos with a detailed description of what is found on disc 1 (always one sided) and what is found on disc 2 (front side and back side). Then when we open the gatefold, we are hit with a panoramic two page sepia photo spread from the movie (a key scene such as the laboratory creation sequence from Frankenstein, the underground crypt sequence with Bela Lugosi as Dracula near his coffin and Claude Rains confronting his son Larry Talbot) housing the two DVDs included in the package. A defining quote from the movie runs along the bottom edge of the inside gatefold. The packaging is extremely impressive and has that expensive "we care" look.

Okay, okay, you agree that the packaging is impressive, but why splurge if we already own the movies? Fine, here's more to consider. Each box set, containing four or five movies (The Wolf Man Box only contains four films), sells for $25 street price at Best Buy (on sale for $20). That rounds out to be $4-$5 per film. But all the extras from previous releases are included, and a marvelous new documentary appears in each box (and each documentary is different for each box set).

First let's examine the *Frankenstein: The Legacy Collection* box set. We get audio commentary on *Frankenstein* and *Bride of Frankenstein*, trailers, *Boo!* a short film, poster and photo archives for *Frankenstein* and *Bride of Frankenstein* and two documentaries. But what is new is the remastered soundtracks on some of the movies which eliminate most of the hiss, pops, crackles and feature a less end-high tinny soundtrack (such remastering is advertised on all three box sets). I have not yet had the time to compare sound between older and newer versions of these movies, but the sound has a heavy bottom and sounds very clean. Unfortunately, the censored grunts and groans of the dying Bela Lugosi from *Dracula*, restored to laserdisc, are once again missing from the soundtrack here. Also a negative splice near the end of the credits for *Frankenstein Meets the Wolf Man*, resulting in an audible, annoying pop, still has not been repaired digitally. But what is new are documentaries hosted by writer/director Stephen Sommers whose new film *Van Helsing* rethinks the original Universal monsters for a new generation. Each documentary in each box focuses on

Finally, *The Wolf Man: The Legacy Collection* box set offers the third and final new Stephen Sommers documentary, this time focusing on lycanthropy. A documentary, *Monster by Moonlight*, appears. Author Tom Weaver provides auditory commentary for *The Wolf Man*.

So, besides getting each movie for at most $5.00, Universal has included all the older extras of insightful and carefully executed documentaries, audio commentaries, poster and still galleries, remastered soundtracks and new documentaries featuring a tie-in to *Van Helsing*. And each collection is housed in attractively designed gatefold boxes that fit inside slipcases.

Still not convinced?????

Here's two more reasons to purchase. The print and soundtrack to *House of Dracula*, first time on DVD, is outstanding. The print barely features a mark and

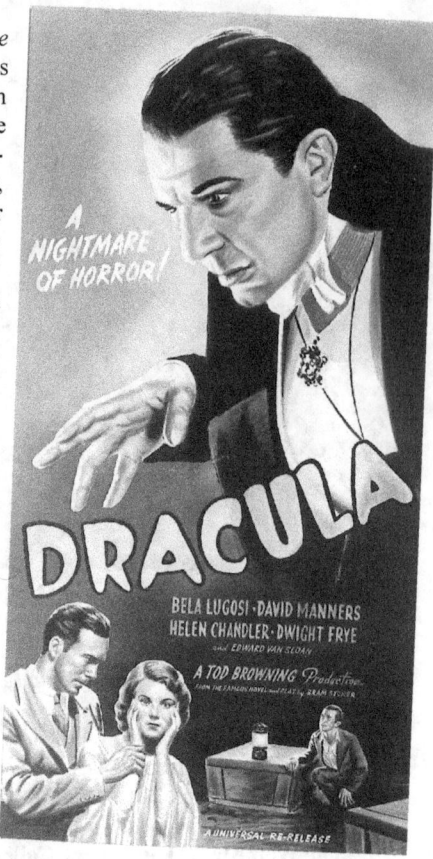

Frankenstein's Monster, The Wolf Man or Dracula. The documentary has on-screen interviews with not only Sommers but members of the cast of *Van Helsing* as well (Kate Beckinsale, Hugh Jackman, etc.) and features impressive montages from all the Universal classics plus footage from *Van Helsing*. As Sommers enthusiastically makes clear, his wish in making *Van Helsing* was to demonstrate that he loved these classic Universal movies.

Dracula: The Legacy Collection box set offers the option of hearing the original minimal *Dracula* musical score or easily switching to the recently-composed Philip Glass score performed by the Kronos Quartet. We also have the *Dracula* Stephen Sommers documentary. Lupita Tovar introduces the Spanish version of *Dracula*, and we have the documentary, *The Road to Dracula*. David J. Skal provides auditory commentary to the original *Dracula*. And we have a poster and still gallery.

the contrast creates true blacks and subtle shades of gray. Most fans consider *House of Dracula* to be perhaps the worst of the monster rally B productions and feel it is inferior to *House of Frankenstein*. What *House of Frankenstein* has is Boris Karloff, but his performance is totally lethargic with J. Carrol Naish stealing the show. John Carradine is good, as is Chaney, Jr., with teenaged Elena Verdugo submitting a fresh performance. But the movie is segmented into parts—the traveling circus, Count Dracula, the Wolf Man and returning Frankenstein's Monster to full potency. For me the film is poorly paced and disappoints. However, *House of Dracula*, directed by Erle C. Kenton, is darker and more shadowy. The plot is fully integrated as one story and Onslow Stevens does a better mad scientist than Karloff did in *House of Frankenstein* (playing a sympathetic Jekyll-Hyde performance). John Carradine is just as effective a Count Dracula here, as is

Lon Chaney, Jr. as Larry Talbot/The Wolf Man. For me *House of Dracula* is the black sheep of the Universal horror factory and its restoration with perfect picture and sound allows fresh evaluations. Don't get me wrong, *House of Dracula* is a B programmer so it does suffer from the same flaws as Universal's other B productions, but I just happen to consider it vastly superior to the generally over-praised *House of Frankenstein*.

Also, the bane of the originally released Universal horror film DVDs has been the subpar print of *Bride of Frankenstein*. Many writers have already pointed out that the laserdisc release was superior in many ways to the well-worn and soft (with less than perfect contrast) DVD release, and most people consider *Bride of Frankenstein* to be the hallmark release of the monster legacy series. However, unannounced, the DVD print of *Bride of Frankenstein* has been quietly upgraded and the result is amazing. Just put in the old DVD release and compare it to this new Legacy box set release. Yes, if one were to quibble, of course one could find flaws in the original source material, and *Bride of Frankenstein* does cry out for the type of restoration accorded *Vertigo* and *Singin' in the Rain*. But the upgraded print provided by Universal is vastly superior to the older DVD print and *Bride of Frankenstein* can once again be seen for the eccentric classic it most certainly is.

Finally, if sales warrant (here's the third and final reason to buy these box sets), Universal intends to perhaps provide Legacy box sets to the Mummy movies, the Creature movies and perhaps other Universal titles that never appeared on DVD. Isn't it about time for *The Black Cat, The Raven* and *The Invisible Ray* to hit DVD!!!! If sales dictate Universal might bring out any number of cherished horror classics (and not just classic releases). So even if you think you have everything included in these three box sets, well, think again. Just like memorable dining experiences that we pay for many times throughout our lifetimes, buying these cherished cinematic classics a second or third time is not insane. I expect to buy them again without complaint, but Universal, please just bring out some new titles as well!

GRAVE DIGGINGS

Dear Gary and Sue:

I have enjoyed reading *Midnight Marquee* 69/70 quite a bit. As I would expect of someone with your knowledge and background, your choices for the top 50 films of the last 40 years are for the most part excellent. There are a few, however, I would quibble with you about.

The Vampire Lovers (1970) is at best mediocre. Its main contribution seems to be making explicit the original novella's sapphic subtext. Still, such a subject is treated far more seriously in *Mulholland Dr.* (where the plot is incomprehensible with such an understanding) or even *Bound* (more crime drama than horror, I grant you, but with some strikingly horrific moments).

Perhaps I enjoy more humor in my horror than you do, but giving place to the shout-a-thon *Day of the Dead* and none to *Return of the Living Dead* (which manages the difficult feat of being both genuinely scary and genuinely funny) seems shortsighted. The third Romero zombie effort does feature a sprightlier pace than *Dawn of the Dead*, but the latter is still wittier and more pointed in its satire.

Much as I enjoy *Twin Peaks*, it is a television series and not a movie, unless you are counting the theatrical version sent overseas which had a different ending.

I love *Ed Wood*, but it is in no way a horror film. Of interest to horror fans, definitely, but it is clearly a highly fictionalized biopic with all the pitfalls that implies. *Shadow of the Vampire*, on the other hand, uses fictionalized versions of real people to make a real horror film about a supposedly real vampire.

If *Ed Wood* qualifies, then why not *Gods and Monsters*? It also would have been nice for there to be a place for an overlooked gem such as *Paperhouse* or *Pitch Black*, and preferring the mixed up *The Frighteners* over the fantastic *Heavenly Creatures* seems a little perverse (though I would agree that Jeffrey Coombs' manic federal agent is a scream and Fox is his usual likable self).

Still, these are quibbles and your suggestions are by and large excellent.

But I am disappointed that you seemed to take the side against *The Wicker Man* over the side for. To me, it seems as if some of the panelists missed the point of the movie, which by and large doesn't take sides. While it is clearly the pagans versus the Christian in this film, the point is more to explicate the beliefs of paganism and how they affront Christian values. Sgt. Howie is called a prig and unsympathetic by some of the panelists, but given what we learn about his values, how else could we expect him to react on an island filled with heathenistic non-believers who may be in a conspiracy to murder an innocent young girl?

Christopher Lee gets all the best lines for a change, so even if it is not one of his biggest parts, it is certainly among his best. Asking the local doctor where the death certificate is seems eminently reasonable behavior—Howie knows these are peculiar people, but a death certificate does have to be signed by a doctor.

The film is set up as a mystery and not a horror film, and doesn't become one until the human sacrifice at the end, though quite a bit of unease is built up as Howie searches for Rowan Morrison, particularly in the longer, fuller cut.

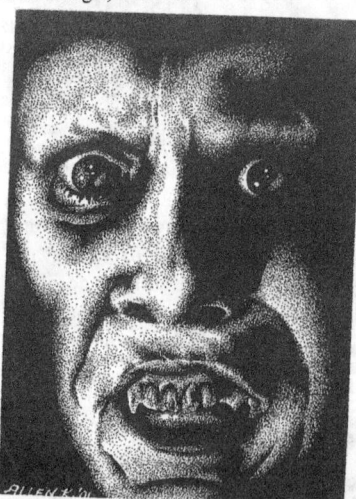

The whole point of the snail scene is not to watch snails copulate, but for Summerisle to express his revulsion at what he sees as hypocrisy—but your panelists don't seem to consider the words being spoken in that scene. Then again, I enjoy the soundtrack to the film quite a bit, and the sexually suggestive lyrics throughout do much to suggest an unrepressed society where sex is considered so natural and out-in-the-open, that young girls are instructed in the phallic symbolism of the maypole ceremony (something that could easily be construed as child abuse in a Christian country).

No one would ever argue that *The Wicker Man* is the scariest horror film ever made, but simple as its narrative is, it is undoubtedly thought provoking.
—Dennis Fischer

[Editor's Note: Dennis, thank you for such a thought provoking letter. I stand by my choices, but perhaps others readers may yet voice their opinions. Thanks for taking the time to comment!]

Dear Midnight Marquee:

I would like to know if your company intends to publish an actor series books on the three most overlooked horror stars: Claude Rains, Henry Hull and Carroll Borland. After looking at all the covers of your magazines in your catalog, I would like to see an issue devoted to the comedy team of Abbott and Costello and their classic movies involving horror stars such as Lugosi, Chaney, Jr., Glenn Strange, John Carradine, etc. Of course *Abbott and Costello Meet Frankenstein* would be the centerpiece of the book. Such a special issue would be a big seller. Not too many magazines are devoted to Bud and Lou and the horror movies they made.

I was happy to receive your catalogue and saw that Lon Chaney, Jr. had his own book. His father overshadowed his son, but most horror fans will remember him as Larry Talbot, the original Wolf Man. Your issue #61 magazine really does him justice. As a loyal customer since 1997, I am always looking forward to seeing your next books or magazines, which cover the horror stars of yesteryear. Forrest J Ackerman made the horror stars come to life in *Famous Monsters*. Other publications such as *Castle of Frankenstein, Monster World, Fantastic Monsters, Mad Monsters, Modern Monsters* did the same.

Sorry to have bothered you, these are only my opinions. Remember, horror mixed with comedy goes a long way!
—Eugene Kirschenbaum

[Editor's Note: Since Carroll Borland only appeared in one horror movie, an entire book devoted to her horror career seems excessive. Same with Henry Hull. However, we are resurrecting our lamented Film Actors Series with Peter Cushing being the featured artist, and the book, edited by our

own Anthony Ambrogio, should be available by the end of the year. More in the series will follow!]

Dear Gary and Susan:

How are the both of you? Just a note thanking you for my recent order... I am enjoying all the back issues of *Midnight Marquee* that you are selling at discount prices. Gary, you should be very proud of your magazine, and just think, you started it when you were only 13 years old! That's simply amazing!! I am an old *Famous Monsters* fan starting with issue #11. In *Midnight Marquee* I most enjoy your reviews of DVDs. I am waiting for your review of the complete collection of *The Twilight Zone* series, also the *Outer Limits* collections. Also, I enjoy the Forgotten Faces articles. I wish you could convince someone like Greg Mank to write a book on Nigel Bruce. The Midnight Marquee/Luminary Press book you published, *Chronicles of Terror: Silent Screams*, is a classic. I highly recommend it. I found information about Chaney, Sr., that I have not seen anywhere else. And Susan, bless her heart, has a wonderful talent for creating very eye-catching covers. I love the *Midnight Marquee Bride of Frankenstein* cover. I am looking forward to the next issue!

—Joseph S. Monistere, Jr.

[Editor's Note: Thank you Joseph for all the kind words. We agree that Silent Screams *is one of the best books published on horror movies that has emerged during the past decade, and it is sadly apparent that there are fewer silent horror film buffs than sound horror buffs, because the sales of the book have been disappointing for such an important work. Even if I were not the publisher, I would still sing the praises of* Silent Screams *and, hopefully, more people will pick up a copy. Fans will* not *be disappointed!]*

Dear Gary and Sue:

Having read and reread Midnight Marquee's 40th Anniversary issue many times, I was surprised that your paragraph (pg. 61) concerning the demise of FANEX had previously escaped me. The event has always been a summer highlight for my wife and me, and judging from attendance, countless others. For those having never attended, FANEX is the model of what a serious horror/fantasy film convention should be.

I hope that the bigger, more extravagant horror conventions are not putting a death knell on FANEX. Your observations on those "dime a dozen" horrorfests is certainly correct. While I did enjoy the Crystal City Monster Rally and Classic FilmFest conventions, these events paled in comparison to the much more erudite and subtle FANEX gatherings. As you stated, these conventions are becoming freak shows staged to make a profit. What do Tracy Lords or the other stars *du jour* have to do with quality horror cinema? And your comments concerning the absence of intellectual panels and discussions is quite accurate. Unfortunately, such junk as *House of 1,000 Corpses* is lauded over the many quality films that define the genre.

FANEX has given horror a legitimate format, and as we fans know, it has never gained the respect it deserves. Your scholarly lectures are stimulating, educational and simply fun to engage in. Friends attended the 2003 FANEX and were mighty impressed, especially concerning the panel of World War I's influence on early horror movies. Plus, where else can you see *The Devil Rides Out* and *Spider Baby* under one roof?

It has taken me too long to subscribe to your fine publication. I pray the FANEX tradition continues. Let the other conventions hawk their Charles Manson tee shirts and porn disguised as something macabre. Your dedication is greatly appreciated by all who share these interests.

—Bill Camp

[Editor's Note: House of 1,000 Corpses *is a little guilty pleasure of mine, but, of course, my heart lies with classic horror. Bill, your kind words are most appreciated about FANEX, a convention that came from the heart, not the wallet. No other current film convention offers what we offered: guest lectures, panel discussions and writer's talks. Other shows might be more successful from the business standpoint, but no show has yet duplicated the purity of spirit that was FANEX. Our favorite shows were those we had before the guests started charging money for their signatures. John Agar, Jeff Morrow, Acquanetta, Veronica Carlson, James Bernard, Freddie Francis, Robert Clarke, William Schallert, Lucille Lund, Jane Adams, Elena Verdugo, et al, were truly wonderful people and really appreciated their FANEX Awards and the sincere appreciation of the FANEX attendees. We have been very lucky to have met so many kind and humble genre legends. It's been a great ride. Thanks again, Bill, your letter meant a lot to both of us, but Sue especially appreciated it!]*

Dear Gary and Sue:

Yes, we now have a DVD and VCR combination player in our living room. I don't intend to replace my tapes, but I'm adding DVDs to go with my VCR collection. However, Universal has tempted me with their new packaging scheme. I definitely like the packaging of the *Dracula*, *Frankenstein* and the *Wolf Man* movies together as box sets. Now, if they would only add *The Mummy* Legacy box set to the series! As I said, I have all of these titles on tape, but like I said earlier, I'm tempted to purchase these DVDs as well.

Thank goodness for Toho! They have finally released their latest "Big G" adventure to our market. It took me a time to get used to the English subtitles, but they are very good DVDs. Their special effects are better than ever. And I must agree that the picture quality is almost movie theater clear. However, I am a little disappointed in that they have changed some of the Godzilla myth around, all of the histories have been changed. In this latest *Godzilla* movie Godzilla and Mothra are both assigned as guardians of Japan, as is Baragon. What's next, Rodan, defender of the universe? So much for my nit picking.

I hope everything is going well for Midnight Marquee. Gary, you and Sue have the best monster film magazine going. I sure enjoy it. Oh, I almost forgot. I watched some of the Van Helsing movie special on the Sci-Fi Channel. Don't know if I will see the movie. It's much too much like Stephen Sommers remake of *The Mummy*. Too much Indiana Jones adventure, with too many James Bond gadgets thrown in.

Hey, just keep Midnight Marquee going. You are appreciated, that's for sure!

—Don Wilhoite

[Editor's Note: Don, thanks for the kind words above. We intend to keep Midnight Marquee *going, even if we may be a little late now that we publish three magazines. First of all, it's about time you switched to DVD. The picture, sound and extras are so fantastic and the cost is cheaper than VHS tapes were even 10 years ago. Keep your tapes until the title is available on DVD, and then make the switch. No reason to not replace your tapes with DVD when DVDs are so cheap. Happy collecting].*

Midnight Marquee—Movie Books for Movie Lovers

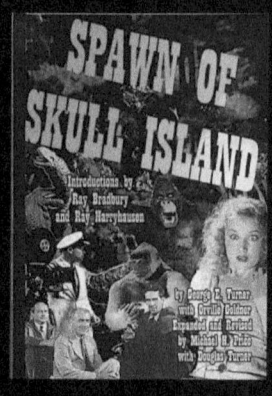

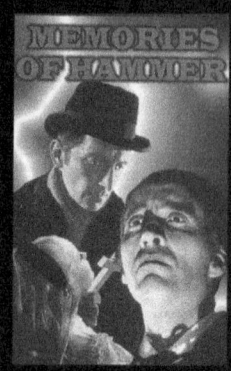

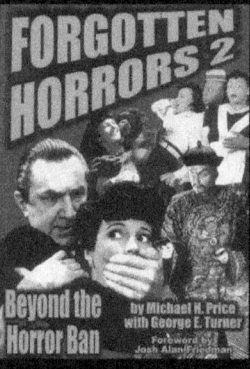

Call 410-665-1198
(9 a.m. -6 p.m. EST)
or e-mail MMarquee@aol.com
for a free catalog

or visit our website at
www.midmar.com
to order books and
magazines

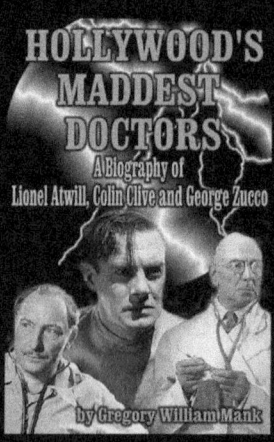

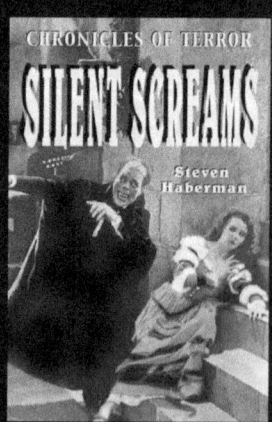

www.ingramcontent.com/pod-product-compliance
Lightning Source LLC
Chambersburg PA
CBHW081728100526
44591CB00016B/2539